Man and the Computer

Man
and the
Computer

John G. Kemeny

Charles Scribner's Sons

New York

Printed in the United States of America
Library of Congress Catalog Card Number 72–1176
AMERICAN MUSEUM OF NATURAL HISTORY
SPECIAL MEMBERS EDITION

Contents

v

Part Two: Symbiotic Evolution

Preface

I was delighted to receive an invitation from the American Museum of Natural History in New York City to deliver the "Man and Nature" lectures in the fall of 1971. It gave me an opportunity to pull together many ideas I have had over the years concerning the impact of computers and their future potential. In spite of the many books dealing with high-speed computers that have been written in recent years, I am convinced that the average intelligent person has little or no understanding of the true nature of a computer or of its power and limitations.

It was not my intention to present an encyclopedic treatment of modern computers, since such treatises are usually thoroughly boring. Since it is too early to write a definitive history of the development of computers, I present instead a personalized view of what has happened in the first twenty-five years of modern computers. From this I go on to a critical evaluation of the present state of the art and the various applications of computers. I conclude with an examination of what seems possible and likely to occur in the next twenty years and a description of several exciting new uses of computers which most of us will live to see.

One common theme runs throughout this book. I believe that next to the original development of general-purpose high-speed computers the most important event was the coming of man-machine interaction. I feel that the true significance of computers in the future will lie precisely in this teamwork of man and computer. We have seen only the early stages of this art and therefore all predictions as to its future impact are highly speculative. I trace much of the criticism and distrust of computer systems to those systems in which computers operate on their own, and I know from personal experience that users who work in a partnership with computers change their attitudes completely. Consequently, the most important applications I see for the future fall into the area of man-machine cooperative systems.

Since the lectures were delivered at the American Museum of Natural History, the temptation to describe this partnership as a "symbiosis" was irresistible. When I first proposed this title I had not yet seen the word used in this context in the literature. Since that time I have seen several such references, for example, in *Computers, System Science, and Evolving Society* by Harold Sackman. While I am sorry that the use of this word is not original with me, I am glad to see that other authors share my feeling that this term from biology appropriately describes the true nature of man-machine interaction.

This book consists of an expanded version of the lectures delivered at the American Museum of Natural History. I am grateful to Charles Scribner's Sons for requiring me to present the material in a form that will be accessible to the nontechnical reader.

I would like to express my thanks to Alexander Fanelli, Stephen Garland, Jennifer Kemeny, and John Mc-Geachie for their reading of this manuscript. I would also like to thank Edward Lathem for his criticism of Chapter 8 and Mrs. Bonnie Clark for the preparation of the manuscript.

Part One

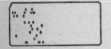

The New Symbiosis

1
A New Species Is Born

H. G. Wells and Julian Huxley in their book *The Science of Life* define symbiosis as "two organisms of different kinds living in intimate union and to the benefit of both." They give a wide variety of fascinating examples starting with lichens in which fungi and algae cooperate, a number of different kinds of plants that have a symbiotic relation with bacteria, cooperation between termites and flagellates, between the hermit crab and the sea anemone, and some less close relations between pairs of animal species. Symbiosis has played an important role in evolution; a 1971 article in *Scientific American* argues that it may have played a decisive role.[1]

It is the theme of this book that within the last generation man has acquired an important symbiote. Man's new partner is the high-speed computer. I intend to explore in detail the present relation between man and computer and to speculate on the role that symbiosis may play in the evolution of both species.

The history of man is well known. The history of his symbiotic partner is not nearly so well known. Therefore I will begin by examining briefly the coming of this "new species."

A Brief History

Modern computers are so new that no definitive history of them has been written, nor shall I attempt one at this time. Instead, I offer a brief personal view of the coming of the modern high-speed computer.

In 1946 I had the privilege of listening to a lecture

4) The New Symbiosis

at Los Alamos by the great Hungarian-born mathematician John von Neumann. I was at that time assigned by the United States Army to work at the Los Alamos computation center. This center consisted of seventeen IBM bookkeeping machines, and a staff of twenty kept the computer going twenty-four hours a day, six days a week. We were solving partial differential equations connected with the design of the atomic bomb. While our operation was no doubt important in the success of the Manhattan project, since these equations could not possibly have been solved by other means, it was very frustrating for twenty people to work around the clock for three weeks to solve one differential equation.

At that time each of our machines was designed to carry out one or two arithmetical operations. For example, one of our better computers could take three numbers A, B, and C, and compute $A \times B + C$. The information was fed to the computers by a deck of IBM cards, each of which contained information about one point in space. The deck of fifty or so cards was fed to the computer, which performed the same operation on each card. The deck was then moved manually to the next machine, which carried the calculations one step further.

A great deal of attention had to be paid to the exact design of how information was distributed on the cards and in what sequence it was carried from machine to machine. The logical control of what a machine did was by means of a plugboard which had to be specially wired for each type of operation. For example, the wiring might indicate that the number A was in columns 1–8, the number B in columns 20–27, the number C in columns 9–15, and the answer was to be put in columns 60–67. When one ran out of space on the cards, the relevant information had to be copied from one card to another by a "reproducer." Finally, at the end of the cycle all the information was summarized on a

5) A New Species Is Born

"tabulator," and this listing was checked manually for catastrophes. If the results looked like utter nonsense, it might have been because a deck had been fed upside down to one of the computers and therefore the entire cycle had to be repeated.

Von Neumann was one of the chief consultants to this computer operation. He must have concluded that even though the work we were doing was useful, with modern technology it should be possible to design computers that would make life a great deal easier. Although I do not have notes on his 1946 lecture, I have never forgotten some of his main points.

VON NEUMANN PROPOSALS

1. Fully Electronic Computers
2. Binary Number System
3. Internal Memory
4. Stored Program
5. Universal Computer

First of all, he argued that the computers of the day, which depended heavily on mechanical parts, were much too slow to be useful. Therefore he proposed an entirely electronic device. He went on to argue that, while the decimal system was perfectly practical for mechanical devices, a binary system would be much easier to implement electronically because of the efficiency of on-off devices. Next he pointed out that if we had faster machines it did not make sense for human beings to have to interfere after each step. Even if a given operation on fifty IBM cards were to be speeded up from a minute to a second, very little would be gained if the cards then had to be manually transferred to another box. Therefore he advocated the existence of an "internal memory" in which partial results could be retained so that the computer could automatically go through many rounds of operations.

Next he pointed out that it is not necessary to build specialized computers for different tasks. The English mathematical logician A. M. Turing had shown that a machine which could carry out a few basic operations could, in principle, carry out any calculation. He therefore proposed that computers be such "universal Turing machines."

His most important proposal, however, concerned the logical control of computers. All of us realized how ridiculous plugboards were as a means for achieving this end. If one was multiplying A by B and then the result by C, one could of course use the same computer. However, since on the second multiplication the information was contained in different columns, the entire plugboard had to be rewired before the cards were reinserted. Von Neumann proposed that one should be able to store a set of instructions within the internal memory of the machine so that the computer could go from step to step by consulting its own memory without waiting for human interference. Such a set of instructions is now known as a "program," and the ability to program computers has been the single major breakthrough that differentiates a modern computer from an old-fashioned business machine.

Of course all the electronic components that von Neumann proposed some twenty-five years ago are now hopelessly out of date, but even the most complex modern machine is based on the principles that he outlined at that time. He was a prophet in predicting the impact of modern computers, but even he underestimated the rapid growth of electronic technology and therefore failed to anticipate the incredible increase in computing power and the impact that the computer would have within a generation.

To one who had just spent a year working on bookkeeping machines, von Neumann's plan sounded like utopia. I fully believed that the dream would be realized, but I wondered if I would live long enough to use one of those magnificent beasts. I did not know that the first fully electronic computer, ENIAC, was even then nearing completion. While it did not incorporate all of von Neumann's principles, a machine built entirely on these principles was constructed under the leadership of von Neumann at the Institute for Advanced Studies in Princeton later in the decade. But massive progress had to wait a few years until the leading bookkeeping machine manufacturer (IBM) decided to take a look at modern computers.

My first chance to use such a computer came in the summer of 1953 when I was a consultant at the Rand Corporation. They had a copy of the prototype built by von Neumann at Princeton (which they christened the JONIAC after the man who was known as "Johnny" to everyone in the profession) and an early IBM 700 series machine. The progress in just seven years was absolutely amazing, and I had no idea that the best was yet to come. I had great fun learning how to program a computer, even though the language used at that time was designed for machines and not for human beings. I once used a computer to check the largest of Lewis Carroll's syllogisms, which involves drawing a conclusion from twelve premises involving thirteen variables. This task would have been completely impossible for the 1946 machines; on a 1953 computer it took a few minutes. For computers today it is a trivial exercise.

I had an interesting experience when I returned to Rand in the summer of 1956. It happened to be one of those years when the government cut back on all research contracts and therefore I was asked to do double duty as a consultant in mathematics and in computing. By then Rand had an IBM 704, which was a fairly powerful modern computer. I drew up a set of recommendations for the improvement of the computation center, only one of which I still remember. I noticed that some of Rand's distinguished and highly paid employees had to hang around for an hour or more to get a five-second shot at the computer. It was a time when computers were very scarce, and very expensive, but a simple cost-effectiveness calculation showed that priorities were being put in the wrong place, to say nothing of the amount of frustration that discouraged the distinguished scientists from using the computer. I therefore recommended a system by which the lengthy computations could be interrupted for a few seconds at a time for someone to check out a program. I would like very much to believe that this recommendation influenced Rand to become one of the pioneers in the development of time-sharing systems. However, I suspect that my recommendation was forgotten and the same conclusion reached independently years later.

We had no computer at Dartmouth College until 1959, but the Massachusetts Institute of Technology was generous enough to let New England college faculty members make use of their computer. I therefore witnessed the coming of the next major breakthrough, the language FORTRAN. It was finally realized that it was much more sensible to teach a machine a language that is easier for human beings to learn than to force every human user to learn the machine's own language. (I have more to say on the subject of language development later in this book.) All of a sudden access to computers by thousands of users became not only possible but reasonable.

While M.I.T. was periodically exchanging its computers for later and more powerful IBM models, incorporating such innovations as transistors and magnetic core memories, Dartmouth finally acquired its first computer in 1959. It was an extremely nice, very small computer, called the LGP-30. By today's standards this machine was tiny and very slow; it took milliseconds rather than microseconds to carry out its computations, and its memory consisted of a single drum. However, for the first time our students acquired hands-on experience with computers, and we were absolutely amazed at the ingenuity and creativeness of a few exceptional undergraduates. Without the experience with the LGP-30 we would never have had the desire or the courage to develop our own time-sharing system.

The story of the coming of the Dartmouth Time-Sharing System is told in Chapter 3. But it is worth noting here how far computers have come in twenty-five years. All the calculations that we did on those seventeen IBM machines at Los Alamos in a full year, a generation ago, can today be carried out by a Dartmouth undergraduate in one afternoon, while a hundred other people are also using the same computer. To me this comparison is more meaningful than simply indicating that calculations that used to take several seconds in 1946 now take several microseconds (millionths of a second).

Computers could remember only a handful of numbers in 1946; today's models can recall hundreds of thousands of numbers instantly. With a somewhat longer delay they have access to a hundred million numbers in their memories. Billions of calculations can be performed in a day, all under the control of internally stored programs that have reached a high degree of sophistication. Perhaps the most remarkable feature of all is that the typical modern computer can carry out several billion calculations a day without making a single mistake.

Although it is easy to see that as computers become more powerful they also become more expensive, it takes a little more sophistication to realize that at the same time the cost of a given computation becomes significantly cheaper each year. James Martin and Adrian R. D. Norman cite some fascinating figures on the exponential growth of computer capabilities and the exponential decline in computer costs. For example, they estimate that in a fifteen-year period the cost of computations decreased by a factor of 1,000.[2]

It is clear that the coming of the computer has both opened up entirely new power to human beings and created vast new problems. Many of these are examined in this book. But the question that interests me most is just what the relationship is between man and computer and how this relationship will influence the evolution of both species. I hope to show that this relationship can fruitfully be viewed as a symbiosis. But is it stretching things too far to consider the computer a new species?

Are Computers a Species?

A species is a distinctive form of life. There is no question that computers are distinctive, but most people would insist rather vehemently that it is ridiculous to compare a machine to a living being. I would like to argue that the traditional distinction between living and inanimate matter may be important to a biologist but is unimportant and possibly dangerously misleading for philosophical considerations.

What distinguishes living from inanimate nature? While there is no universally accepted definition of life, the following six criteria usually enter such a definition:

1. Metabolism, the ability to perform a chemical change in matter to generate energy
2. Locomotion (not a universal criterion)
3. The ability to reproduce itself
4. Individuality
5. In higher animals, intelligence (the ability to think and to communicate)
6. That it is a "natural" as opposed to an "artificial" being

11) A New Species Is Born

Modern thinking about life has been strongly influenced by Charles Darwin. We tend to shape our definition of "living" to fit those species that have evolved on earth through the evolutionary process. Since the highest species tend to have all the characteristics of lower ones, plus additional ones, the definition puts particular stress on lower living forms in order to be as inclusive as possible. Since metabolism is common to all species while intelligence is not, the former is considered an essential trait for life, while the latter is a luxury. In the classification no provision has been made to include species that demonstrate some of the higher qualifications but not the lower ones, since examples of such species are not found in the evolutionary chain. I suspect that extraterrestrial exploration will discover species that biologists will be forced to classify as living even though they do not fit the standard definition. Traditional definitions are already in a great deal of trouble since the discovery of viruses and the rapid development of biochemical laboratories.

How well do computers fit the definition? First, there is no question in my mind that they are intelligent. They show the ability to think and to communicate in any scientifically testable sense. They can carry out arithmetical and verbal tasks. They can follow a long sequence of logical argument. They can ask and answer questions. They learn rapidly and remember well. They could be programmed to do well on intelligence tests.

Second, they show individuality in the very same sense that living beings do. This alone I would consider sufficient justification for treating them as a new species. I would like to point out, however, that several other criteria could be met with very little trouble.

People are, of course, put off by the fact that today's computers don't at all fit their image of a living being. However, it would not be difficult in the next decade to make a quite powerful robot. This could look on the exterior very much like a human being, or like a dog or a cat, if preferred. Miniaturization of parts makes possible the construction of a quite powerful computer about the size of the human brain. It would be very simple to provide the robot with primitive sense organs and with a means for locomotion. It could then react to sight and sound stimuli and move about in a manner perhaps not as graceful as that of a cat or even of a human being, but still much better than many living species.

The problem of providing a metabolic mechanism for the robot is also easy to solve. If it is equipped with a power cell and instructed to go periodically to an electric outlet and plug itself in to recharge its batteries, that would constitute metabolism. I don't see why metabolism has to be limited to chemical rather than physical processes. However, for traditionalists, I suggest that the robot could absorb light as a source of energy and use it to convert ordinary food through chemical processes.

The skeptic next brings up the question of reproduction. This is actually one of the simplest problems to solve. Von Neumann demonstrated early in the development of computers the theoretical possibility of a self-reproducing machine.[3] But given the potentialities of robots that could exist by 1980, there are much simpler solutions for the problem of reproduction. After all, what is reproduction? It is the ability to take raw materials from the environment and put them together in a manner that will make a rough duplicate of the organism itself. Truly there is no difficulty in principle in having a robot assemble a new robot. When it has physically assembled the new machine, it could transfer to it the contents of its own memory (a familiar process in computation centers) and push the button that turns on the new robot. I feel certain that this procedure would meet most definitions of reproduction.

When the skeptic is pressed to the wall he usually falls back on the fact that machines are "artificial" or "man-made" and therefore do not qualify as "natural" living beings. But this is a distinction that is becoming increasingly difficult to maintain. Man is very close to synthesizing living beings in the biological laboratories. These, although clearly man-made, will be indistinguishable from living beings created in nature. Besides, once there are robots that reproduce themselves, only the first one will be man-made; the others would be created by their "parents." It would be easy to program a reproducing robot so that each offspring differs slightly from its parents, and it would probably be a good idea to let each robot figure out some improvement in its offspring so that an evolutionary process can take place.

Whether the skeptic accepts this argument or not, I hope I have shown that modern computers demonstrate the ability to think, to remember, and to communicate with the outside world. In these capacities they are sufficiently like species of living beings to justify considering a possible symbiotic relationship between man and the computer.

2
What Each Species Contributes

In forming a partnership it is important to consider what special skills each partner can contribute. I will first consider the computer and then man, leading up to the question of how the two can best collaborate. That question is considered again in Chapter 4.

The Computer

The single most important feature of a modern computer is its incredible speed. As a rough rule of thumb a computer is a million times as fast as a human being. Using the usual terminology, this means that it improves on man's ability to carry out a variety of routine tasks by six orders of magnitude (that is, ten to the sixth power).

Its second most important feature is its incredible memory. Von Neumann realized twenty-five years ago that the truly high speed computer would be of little use unless it had a memory sufficient both in capacity and in speed. It is the high-speed memory of the computer that enables it to receive and retain a long list of instructions and to consult these instructions without slowing down the rate of computations. This memory is also used to retain all the partial calculations that are necessary to complete an argument that may be millions or even billions of steps long.

The fact that expensive high-speed memory is now supplemented by even larger, but less expensive memories that are still very fast compared to human processes, enables modern computers to work with incredible amounts of information. For example, all the information in the *Encyclopaedia Britannica* can be stored in the memory of a modern computer, and any page of the *Encyclopaedia* can be retrieved in a fraction of a second.

In the early days of computing it was feared that computers beyond a certain size and a certain speed would become useless because of the high probability of error. Even with the best technology available to the early designers of computers, the probability was too high that in millions of steps, using millions of pieces of information, the computer would make one mistake which would ruin the result. These fears proved groundless. Reliability of electronic components has improved even more rapidly than the size and speed of machines, so that the probability of a single error in an entire day of operations is much smaller today than it was fifteen years ago. For most ordinary users it is perfectly safe to assume that if the computer produces a reasonable answer, it is the correct one. If errors are made, they tend to be of catastrophic proportions, as when the computer has what can only be described as a nervous breakdown. The symptoms of this are so obvious that if they occur in the midst of a computation we know that the results will have to be recalculated. A random undetectable error is almost unheard of.

A very important attribute of the high-speed computer is its ability to learn and to remember indefinitely what it has learned. To take advantage of the power of the computer one must teach it a variety of procedures by means of programs. A program may consist of three instructions or 300,000, depending on the complexity of the task. The design of a program of several thousand instructions is a complicated and time-consuming task for human beings, but once this program has been taught to the computer, it can be expected to remember it forever and carry it out in an errorless fashion.

The computer is the most patient and obedient servant that man has ever found. As long as it is well cared for, so that its physical well-being is assured, it will serve him well. The computer's sole goal in life is to carry out instructions given to it by human beings. A favorite joke about high-speed computers goes somewhat as follows: "The trouble with old-fashioned computers was that they never did what you told them to do. The trouble with modern computers is the fact that they do precisely what you told them to do, and not what you meant to tell them to do." In other words, computers are so obedient that, even if the instructions you give them are completely nonsensical, the computer will carry them out to the letter.

Such a computer, operating in the time-sharing mode described in Chapter 3, can communicate simultaneously with hundreds of human beings, irrespective of where they are located, and carry out an incredible variety of tasks at a speed so great that each user has the illusion that the full service of the computer is available to him.

Man

After all this praise of the computer it is not unreasonable to ask whether man has anything useful to contribute to the partnership. Fortunately there are a number of areas in which human beings are indispensable, either because man does not know how to carry the task out with the computer alone, or because man seems to have certain talents which the computer does not share.

Since modern computers were originally designed to

carry out mathematical calculations, one would think that, at least in this area, they would have replaced human beings completely. But this is far from being true. Man has a talent for recognizing subtle patterns that lead to short cuts. While most experts are convinced that computers can be taught this talent, very little progress has been made in this area. One can't help reaching the conclusion that it is more efficient to use a human being as the computer's partner than to spend many years trying to teach the computer a talent for which it is not well suited.

For example, although computers can now create mathematical proofs, they are extremely bad at it. Distinguishing one geometrical shape from another is a trivial task for a human being but appears to be immensely complicated for computers. (Thus a computer that does spectacularly on an intelligence test for sixteen-year-olds might do badly on a test designed for six-year-olds.) While a great deal of publicity was given to the power of computers to translate from one language into another, progress has been painfully slow.

Second, it took the development of computer memories to show just how remarkably good human memory is. According to the best estimates, man's memory still exceeds that of the largest existing computer. And although we operate at speeds that are painfully slow compared to the basic cycle of a high-speed computer, we are remarkably efficient at retrieving items from our memory. We seem to be able to do it through mysterious processes of association that no one has duplicated on a computer. How does one associate a phrase in a book with a conversation held ten years ago? How does one associate a smell with a childhood memory? How, in trying to solve a problem, do we pull out three unrelated memories going back to different periods in our life to come up with a new approach to the solution? And how do we sift through hopelessly large amounts of information presented to us daily by our senses and retain just the most relevant facts?

It is important to recognize that, while computers are magnificent beasts, they are in many respects very stupid. While they are excellent at carrying out complex instructions at tremendously high speed and with great accuracy, they are completely lacking in judgment and in common sense. If you tell a computer to carry out a million calculations but do not tell it to print the answer, it will reach the solution to the problem, but you will never know what it is. Partway through its calculations it may get into a hopeless tangle. At this point a human being could abandon the approach and try a new attack, but the computer cannot distinguish one set of numbers from another and will merrily grind on with its totally useless computations. In short, it has no way of evaluating its work. While some degree of evaluation can be built into a sophisticated computer program, I am convinced that in complex tasks it is better to have the computer file periodic progress reports and let a human being do the evaluation.

Men also have mysterious talents which are vaguely described as intuition and creativity. No one has yet succeeded in translating the talent for fruitful hunches into a computer program. While a computer has a great advantage in that it can try a thousand alternatives in the time that a man is trying half a dozen, it is not uncommon that by a good intuitive guess the man succeeds in half a dozen trials while the computer fails in a thousand random attempts.

I therefore see man as contributing several essential talents to the symbiotic relationship. Man should decide the best use of computers. Man should set the goals and tell the computer how to work toward them. It is best for man to monitor the work of the computer so that he may use his powers of intuition and evaluation to guide it in its work. In short, while 99.99 percent of the work will be done by the computer, the 1/100 percent assigned to human beings is an essential contribution to the partnership.

Working Together

From the preceding description it would appear that man and computer complement each other beautifully. Yet the difference between man and computer is much greater than that between any pair of partners in a symbiotic relationship in nature. Therefore the partnership does not function as simply and inevitably as it does in such observed relationships.

Perhaps it would have been better if man could have designed machines which were only a thousand times as fast as human beings but had a little bit of common sense. Then, in writing a program, it would not be necessary to spend endless hours worrying about all the things that can go wrong without the computer's realizing it. Perhaps it would have been wise to settle for a less efficient electronic memory but one that operated on principles closer to man's. But since we do not understand how human memory works, we must settle for enormous volume and great speed combined with lack of sophistication. For example, although, as already mentioned, the entire *Encyclopaedia Britannica* can be stored within the memory of the computer, when the machine is told to find the article on "Mammals" it is a wise precaution to tell it not to start at the beginning of the *Encyclopaedia* but to go first to the letter M. Storing the information is easy, but to construct an index that will enable the computer to find an individual item as quickly as a human being can find it by turning to the right page requires a degree of sophistication that at the moment only humans can exercise. The facts that all twenty-four volumes have been stored and any page can be retrieved in a small fraction of a second without error are not very helpful as long as it takes the computer an hour to find the right page.

I am convinced, however, that the combination of human intuition and creativity with the computer's ability to learn and to remember all that it has been taught will lead to solutions of these problems. The next considerations are the way the man-machine relationship works and what we can hope from it when the two species learn to work together.

3
Time Sharing

A New Relationship

During the 1960s a fundamental change occurred in the relationship of man to computer. This new relationship is known technically as "time sharing." A small number of experimental time-sharing systems were developed in the first half of the decade, and during the second half time-sharing systems spread like wildfire. It is only through this new development that a true symbiotic relationship between man and computer is possible.

For the first two decades of the existence of high-speed computers, machines were so scarce and so expensive that man approached the computer the way an ancient Greek approached an oracle. A man submitted his request to the machine and then waited patiently until it was convenient for the machine to work out the problem. There was a certain degree of mysticism in the relationship, even to the extent that only specially selected acolytes were allowed to have direct communication with the computer. While computers solved many problems that were previously beyond man's power, true communication between the two was impossible.

In the original mode of using computers, known as "batch processing," hundreds of computer requests were collected by the staff of a computation center and then fed to the machine in a "batch." The computer took the problems one at a time, worked on one, wrote the answer on a magnetic tape, and immediately turned to the next. When a given batch session was completed, the answers were printed from the tape and distributed to the human users. This was considered an extremely efficient use of the computers, since the machines never had to wait for the next problem. However, to paraphrase the famous mathematician Norbert Wiener, it was a rather inhuman use of human beings. The typical user had to wait twenty-four hours to receive the solution of his problem. But if the problem would have taken him years to solve by himself, and if he indeed received a solution, he was perfectly happy.

The shortcoming of batch processing is the simple fact that most computer runs do not result in the solution to a problem, but in the detection of errors or in the printing of completely wrong answers. The typical user may need ten to twenty trial attempts before his program works correctly. A single run of a program may result in the detection of two or three errors, perhaps as simple as the mistyping of a given word. Since it takes the computer a fraction of a second to detect simple errors, managers of computing centers claimed that batch processing was highly efficient. However, if each such trial run delayed the user by twenty-four hours, it typically took two or three weeks for him to produce a correct program. It was most frustrating for the average user to have to wait twenty-four hours to learn that his program contained a small typographical or logical error. While batch processing is completely efficient from the point of view of keeping the machine busy at all times, it is most inefficient from the human point of view.

I recall a debate that I had in the mid-1960s with the director of a famous computation center. He was giving a report on the efficiency of his computer system, including statistics on how much computing time the average user needed. He indicated that the users were on the whole extremely happy with the service they received. My rebuttal was: "The average computer user never uses your system at all because he finds it too frustrating." At the time that I made this statement it was an intuitive evaluation of potential computer users, but my prediction has been completely borne out by experience with good time-sharing systems.

Many important computer applications that would take a human being several months of hard work can be accomplished by a machine in less than a second. As a matter of fact, most computer applications probably fall into this range. Although the typical user would love to have his problem solved by the computer, he is not willing to make daily pilgrimages to the center just to find out that he has made another error. What he would like is to have a computer of his own, which he can use privately at his own convenience, correcting his ten to twenty errors in one session and not quitting until he has obtained his results.

It is this challenge that was met by the development of time sharing. In a time-sharing system a hundred individuals all use the same computer at the same time, in complete privacy, and enjoy the illusion that the computer's sole purpose is to help them. The goal is accomplished by using the tremendous differential in speed between the computer and man to allow the computer to process "simultaneously" a hundred different requests. The result is great efficiency in computer use, with a vastly different effect on human beings. An accidental but all important by-product of time sharing is man-machine communication.

Since an understanding of time-sharing systems is crucial for the remainder of this book, I will describe one such system in detail.

The Dartmouth Time-Sharing System

In 1963 Dartmouth College decided to make an introduction to the use of computers a regular part of the

Liberal Arts program. Some 90 percent of the last seven freshman classes, or over 700 students a year, have received computer training.

It was clear from the beginning that the implementation of this goal was impossible in a batch-processing system. The thought of several hundred students juggling their academic schedules so that they might come each day to the computation center to receive the latest computer output and then waiting several weeks for their first program to work correctly was an educational nightmare. Therefore Dartmouth became one of the pioneers of time sharing. A team consisting of two faculty members and a group of undergraduate research assistants developed a prototype time-sharing system which became operational in the fall of 1964. Since that time that system has been commercially marketed by General Electric Company all over the world. This led to a joint effort by Dartmouth College and General Electric for the development of a much larger and more ambitious time-sharing system. Although the two institutions eventually took different paths, out of the joint effort came GE's present Mark II Time-Sharing System and the current Dartmouth Time-Sharing System (DTSS).

The diagram on page 25 is a schematic representation of DTSS, or indeed of almost any time-sharing system. Each user is provided with a terminal of his own. This may be a typewriterlike device, or a cathode-ray tube with a keyboard, or any one of several other available terminals. The terminal is linked to the computation center through an ordinary telephone line and therefore its location is irrelevant. Today some 200 terminals are linked to DTSS, and although most of them are on the Dartmouth campus, there are a great many spread all over the northeastern United States and eastern Canada. Demonstrations of the system, using Dartmouth's Kiewit Computation Center, have been given

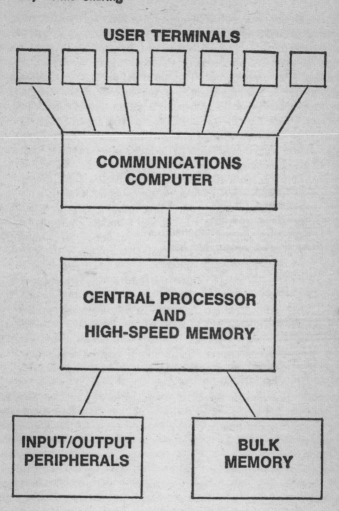

USER TERMINALS

COMMUNICATIONS COMPUTER

CENTRAL PROCESSOR AND HIGH-SPEED MEMORY

INPUT/OUTPUT PERIPHERALS

BULK MEMORY

The Dartmouth Time-Sharing System

all over this country and one was given in Edinburgh, Scotland.*

The user types in his problem on his terminal, the problem is processed at the computation center, and error messages or solutions are typed out on his terminal immediately. One secret of the success of this system is the fact that the actual computation time is very small compared to the time it takes to type a program or to have answers printed out. For this reason the terminals are not connected directly to the main computer (central processor) but to an inexpensive communications computer. In a typical session the user will spend several minutes typing in a program before he makes his first request to the central processor. During this time he is tying down only his share of the communications computer and this inexpensive machine can handle communications with all terminals simultaneously. The request may then require a fraction of a second or a few seconds of computing time, after which the central processor sends the results or error messages to the communications computer, which types them out on the user's terminal.

The first few results will of course be error messages or erroneous answers. Time sharing has not reduced the number of errors that a typical human being makes. However, as soon as the user receives an error message he can type in a correction and try to run his program again. Instead of a turnaround time of twenty-four hours, only one minute is usually required. Obviously

* This demonstration was given by Dr. Myron Tribus, at that time Dean of the Thayer School at Dartmouth College, later U.S. Assistant Secretary of Commerce, and currently a vice president of the Xerox Corporation. He used an ordinary terminal attached to the transatlantic cable and typed the problems in Edinburgh; they were solved in Hanover, New Hampshire, and the solutions were printed out in Edinburgh within seconds.

the communications computer plays a crucial role; most of the time either the user is typing or the results are being typed, and therefore only the secondary machine is tied down.

Nevertheless, with a hundred simultaneous users, several will be asking for computer services at the same time. A given central processor can work on only one problem at a time. However, it is programmed to work in a simple round robin, assigning to each active user a fraction of a second of computing time. If the machine quickly finds an error, the small "shot" may be sufficient to diagnose the trouble. Then the processor sends to the communications computer a suitable error message and forgets about that particular user, turning to the remaining customers.

If the program is correct and requires a substantial amount of computation time, the central processor gives the customer his current share, saves all the computations, and turns to the next user. Soon, perhaps only a second later, it is again the turn of the customer to get additional computation time; he gets as many shots at the computer as are necessary to complete the program. In a well-tuned time-sharing system the user who needs a second or less of computation time should receive an output within ten seconds; indeed, responses within two or three seconds are quite common. Since it is very difficult for the human mind to adjust to the fact that within ten seconds the computer may have serviced a hundred requests, the customer has the illusion that he has sole use of the machine.

The central processor has a bulk memory available for two different purposes. Part of the bulk memory is earmarked as "scratch paper." As the user builds up his program it is stored in this scratch area until a request for processing is received. Again, when the central processor finds that it is not able to complete the user's request in a fraction of a second, it writes out partial results in the scratch area, so that the next time it is that user's turn it may continue where it left off. It also uses the scratch area as a buffer (temporary storage space) from which it feeds computed results to the communications processor.

Most of the bulk memory, however, is available for the storage of user programs. This is one of the great luxuries of a time-sharing system. The user may at any time request that one of his programs be saved for future use. If he returns the next day or the next month he may, by typing a single line, retrieve his program exactly as he left it. This is highly advantageous both for the repeated use of the same program and for saving a program that is not working quite correctly so that the user may take time to think about his problem. In addition, the bulk memory has available a large collection of "library programs" which any user may call upon to solve a variety of standard problems. For example, a user who wishes to execute any one of many standard statistical tests can simply call a program from this collection, supply his own data, and then ask the machine to analyze his data. This brings a variety of mathematical techniques within the grasp of a user who would not have been able to write these programs himself.

Finally, the time-sharing system has available a number of input/output peripherals for the handling of punch cards and magnetic tapes and for the printing of bulk results on the high-speed printer. These peripherals are important for system maintenance and for an occasional very large job, but most users have no need for them since their personal terminal serves all their needs.

This completes the schematic description of a time-sharing system; for the reader interested in technical details a complete description of DTSS is given later in this chapter.

A Language for Communication

It has often been said that verbal communication by means of speech or writing is the single most important ability that distinguishes man from lower species. If communication within a given species is so crucial, it is all the more important between two species as different as man and the computer.

Built into computers is a language known as "machine language." It is a natural language for an electronic computer since each instruction corresponds to simple electronic circuitry, but it is most unnatural for a human being to learn. In the early years of computers, when human beings were forced to write their programs in machine language, computer programming was an art restricted to a handful of experts. Therefore the invention of the language called FORTRAN was a major advance.

FORTRAN combines words from ordinary English with simple mathematical symbols in a language which, although artificial, is so designed that it can be easily learned by a human being. A computer as constructed by the manufacturer does not know FORTRAN. Therefore a group of experts must first write long series of instructions (typically many thousands of instructions) in machine language, which teach the machine how to speak FORTRAN. (Since time sharing gives the illusion of carrying on a conversation with the computer, one commonly refers to computers as "speaking" certain languages.) Once this task has been accomplished, a computer that has been fed this specific program speaks FORTRAN without ever making a mistake. Then any user who learns to write a program in FORTRAN can communicate freely and easily with the computer. Indeed, the computer has no difficulty in learning a wide variety of such languages; all that is required is to feed in a special program that explains the language to the computer.

While the availability of FORTRAN extended computer usage from a handful of experts to thousands of scientific users, we at Dartmouth envisaged the possibility of millions of people writing their own computer programs. Therefore, we decided to design a new computer language that would be accessible to typical college students. This is how the language called BASIC was created. Profiting from years of experience with FORTRAN, we designed a new language that was particularly easy for the layman to learn and that facilitated communication between man and machine.

In the design of artificial languages there is a tendency to build in all kinds of complications so that the experts may more easily write complicated programs. We resisted this temptation. We first designed a few simple instructions for the lay user, to enable him to write his first few computer programs with very little training. Dartmouth freshmen listen to two one-hour lectures and then read a short manual. Before the end of the first week of the course, the typical student is able to write at least one usable program. For the rest of the term his learning experience consists entirely of sitting at a terminal and typing in and "debugging" his own programs.

Each student, during a ten-week term, must write four test programs entirely on his own and work on them until they are errorless. Once a student thinks that his program is correct, he submits it for testing by the computer. The machine will give him either an official approval of his program or a hint as to where there is a mistake. This simple training system has been successfully in operation for seven years, and to the best of my knowledge not one student who has tried it has failed

to complete most or all of the test programs. Therefore we have demonstrated that with a language as simple as BASIC computer programming is not beyond
the competence of any intelligent human being.

The secret of BASIC is the fact that it is written on
several levels. While over the years many advanced features have been added, so that BASIC is as effective as
any other computer language now in common use, the
novice may still restrict his programming to level one,
which is no more complicated than it was in 1964. Each
new level has been added in the form of additional op-
tions to be learned as the user finds a need for them,
but no new level is ever added at the price of compli-
cating the more elementary levels.

The following program shows how simple BASIC is.
It is designed to compute the square roots of numbers
from 20 through 30:

```
1  For N = 20 to 30
2  Print N, SQR(N)
3  Next N
4  End
```

The first line instructs the computer to let N stand,
successively, for the integers from 20 through 30. Line
2 results in the printing of the number N and of its
square root. (The abbreviation "SQR" is used since
there is no square-root sign on a teletypewriter.) At
line 3 the computer goes on to the next value of N,
until the task is completed. Then it reaches line 4 and
stops.

Since BASIC is the first language to have been written since the invention of time sharing, a means for
direct communication between computer and human
being was written into the language. At any point in his
program the user may request that the computer type
out partial results on the user's terminal. The computer
may then be instructed to ask certain questions so that

the user can instruct the machine on how it should proceed. These "interactive programs" may in the long run prove to be the greatest asset of time sharing. Examples of uses of interactive programs are given in the next section.

Time sharing has a number of obvious advantages over batch processing. The user may sit at the terminal and work until his problem is solved. He does this in complete privacy, so that no one ever knows how many mistakes he made before he obtained the correct results. This psychological factor is of overwhelming importance. While many students could have mastered computers even without this guaranteed privacy, most faculty members would have refused to expose themselves to the embarrassment of publicly committing hundreds of mistakes before they became experts. The availability of a language as simple as BASIC has made the learning task so simple that computers have come within the power of every intelligent human being, and time sharing has made it possible to have direct communication between man and machine.

Some Typical Uses of Time Sharing

Before the coming of time sharing only a negligible fraction of faculty and students at Dartmouth had ever used a computer. Seven years later 90 percent of all students know how to use a computer, and most of them make use of the machine freely throughout their college careers. In addition, well over half of the faculty uses it at one time or another.

In a typical day more than a thousand different people take advantage of the time-sharing system. On campus this is accomplished from any one of 150 different terminals located in twenty-five different buildings. In addition, DTSS serves as a regional computation center for New England; some twenty-five secondary schools and twenty-five colleges are connected with the computing center on a full-time basis, and many other colleges and high schools use it occasionally for demonstrations or experiments. It is not surprising that the departments of mathematics, natural sciences, and engineering are all heavy users of the computation center. More unexpectedly, however, the heaviest users are actually the students in business administration and some of the social sciences. There have also been a number of exciting applications of the computer in the humanities and in medicine. Computer applications now pervade the entire curriculum.

The computation center is run in a manner analogous to Dartmouth's million-volume open-stack library. Just as any student may go in and browse in the library or check out any book he wishes without asking for permission or explaining why he wants that particular book, he may use the computation center without asking permission or explaining why he is running a particular program. This freedom of usage has greatly contributed both to the popularity of DTSS on campus and to its wide usage. A survey shows that the average undergraduate spends slightly over one hour a week at the computer terminal. Of course, the word "average" is misleading, as usual, in that a student may spend several hours a week there in one term when he has to do a major project for one of his courses and may not use the terminal at all during another part of the year.

More than half of the total computing time is devoted to course assignments. Since practically all students know how to use the computer, it has become a matter of routine to give computer homework assignments in a wide variety of courses. In a physics course, where traditionally a student would have demonstrated the operation of Newton's Laws by calculating manually what happens when one billiard ball hits another one, the student will now write a computer program to plan a rocket trip to the moon. In mathematics courses a wide variety of algorithms (or computational techniques) traditionally illustrated by trivial applications can now be applied to realistic problems by means of the computer. An engineering student will be able to do serious engineering design problems as an undergraduate. Social scientists have access to million-item data files for use in statistical research or in testing hypotheses. Business administration students have at their fingertips a tool more powerful than that available to the average business executive. Therefore, classroom applications may vary from problems as simple as a compound-interest calculation or the plotting of a graph to significant term projects which in an earlier day would have qualified as high-level research.

In fact, DTSS, although originally designed purely for educational purposes, is a powerful research tool. Hundreds of faculty members who a decade ago would never have dreamed of using a computer now use it routinely. A large number of undergraduate and graduate students have lucrative computer-programming assistantships in which they help faculty members on research problems.

In addition to classroom and research uses there is a great deal of recreational use of DTSS. The computer library contains a wide variety of games, most of them written by students. An old favorite is the football game, in which the user quarterbacks the Dartmouth team while the computer plays the dual role of quarterbacking the opposing team and of simulating nature (that is, figuring out by means of specified probabilities what actually happens). Since computers are very good at imitating chance events, the program results in a highly realistic simulation of a true football game. Even if the user called the same play under the same circumstances every time, no two games would ever be alike. A long pass thrown on third down from a given position on the field may once result in a thirty-yard completion while the next time it is attempted it may result in an incompletion, an interception, or in the passer's being thrown for a loss. There are simulated games in a wide variety of sports as well as games that teach bidding at bridge or allow the user to gamble against a computer for imaginary stakes.

At Dartmouth we do not consider these recreational uses frivolous. First of all, they are an important resource for relaxation in a residential college environment. But, more importantly, for many inexperienced users the opportunity of playing games against a computer is a major factor in removing psychological blocks that frighten the average human being away from free use of machines. Indeed, we are proud of the fact that one of the places that Dartmouth students take their dates to "show off" is the computation center. While they are likely to play several games there, they are also quite likely to show off with programs that they themselves have written.

Although many of the applications described here are straightforward computations which could be done in a batch-processing system, there are also many that make essential use of the communications capabilities of the time-sharing system. For example, when a user calls for a library program, he will receive instructions from the computer on how the program is to be used. In many library programs the computer from time to time asks the user for key pieces of information which it needs to solve the specified problem. None of the games would be possible without the time-sharing system. In the football game, every time Dartmouth has the ball, the computer first asks the user what play he wants to call and then informs him of the results. During a typical session, which takes fifteen minutes, the user may have a chance to call some thirty plays and receive the re-

DARTMOUTH FOOTBALL

(The numbers following "NEXT PLAY?" were typed by the user.)

LONG PASS. INCOMPLETE. NO GAIN
BALL ON YALE 20 YARD LINE
DOWN 3   YARDS TO GO: 12

QUICK KICK. 38 YARD PUNT
BALL ON DARTMOUTH 42 YARD LINE
FIRST DOWN DARTMOUTH ***

NEXT PLAY? 3
SHORT PASS. COMPLETE. 10 YARD GAIN
BALL ON YALE 48 YARD LINE
FIRST DOWN DARTMOUTH ***

NEXT PLAY? 2
TRICKY RUN. 10 YARD GAIN
BALL ON YALE 38 YARD LINE
FIRST DOWN DARTMOUTH ***

NEXT PLAY? 4
LONG PASS. COMPLETE. 31 YARD GAIN
BALL ON YALE 7 YARD LINE
FIRST DOWN DARTMOUTH ***

NEXT PLAY? 1
SIMPLE RUN. 1 YARD GAIN
BALL ON YALE 6 YARD LINE
DOWN 2   GOAL TO GO

NEXT PLAY? 2
TRICKY RUN. TOUCHDOWN ***
KICK IS GOOD

SCORE: 7 TO 0

sults of these as well as the plays called by the opposing team. It should be noted that while football takes fifteen minutes to play, most of this time is taken up by the computer's typing out the results of plays; less than two seconds of computing time is used. The fact that the human being can receive excellent (and highly entertaining) service for fifteen minutes while using less than two seconds of computing time of course explains how DTSS can accommodate well over one hundred users simultaneously.

Quite recently a new capability was added to DTSS. It is now possible to connect two or more human beings to the same computer program. This enables them to work on the same problem simultaneously and to communicate via the computer. The earliest application of this has been to games. There is now a version of the football game in which two different people sit at their own terminals and quarterback the opposing teams. While one of them calls offensive signals, the other calls defensive signals. A number of educational uses of this multiteletype hookup, such as business games and small group experiments, have been considered, but so far we have only the vaguest impressions as to the full power of a team consisting of several human beings and a computer.

A Technical Description of DTSS

For the benefit of those interested in the technical details of a time-sharing system, this section describes DTSS from that standpoint. The reader who is not interested in such details may skip to the next section without losing the continuity of the book.

I will begin by describing the equipment that is schematically shown in the diagram on page 25. In indicating the sizes of various memories I will use as a basic unit a "word" of thirty-six "bits" (0's or 1's); such a word can hold either a computer instruction, a nine-digit number, or a word of six letters.

There is a wide variety of user terminals available in DTSS. The commonest one is a model 33 teletype, which is widely used in many businesses. This is the slowest but least expensive device. It can type at a maximum speed of ten characters a second. Various faster and fancier terminals are available, including type-writers that type at fifteen to thirty characters a second and provide upper- and lower-case capabilities, and even faster terminals, usually of the cathode-ray-tube type. It is also possible to connect a pen-and-ink plotter to an ordinary terminal so that more accurate drawings of graphs may be obtained as part of a computer run.

The communications computer consists of two GE Datanet-30s, each with its own 8000 word memory. Approximately half of the memory in each Datanet-30 is devoted to the program that instructs the Datanet in how to handle various communications terminals. The remainder of the memory serves to buffer input and output messages. A total of 160 lines are connected to the two Datanets, although we have never used that many simultaneously. The record usage so far has been 120 lines, but we know that 120 simultaneous users do not completely load the system.

The "central processor" consists of two GE (now Honeywell) 635s. These are powerful modern com-puters; one of them serves as the "master processor" and the other in "slave mode." This means that the latter is forced to obey the commands of the former. The mas-ter processor carries out all executive functions, the most important ones being the scheduling of user jobs and the allocation of high-speed memory to them. All the time of the slave computer and about half that of the master computer is available for the processing of user jobs. The high-speed memory consists of 160,000 words with a basic cycle time of one microsecond.

The bulk memory consists of two entirely different components, one of which is a high-speed drum with three-quarters of a million words. This is the "scratch paper" referred to in the schematic description. Long-range storage is handled by two IBM 2314s with a total capacity of 72 million words.

The peripherals include a card reader and a card punch which are used very little in DTSS. There are six tape handlers which are used primarily for safekeeping of information. There is also a very good 1200-line-a-minute printer which is used for bulk outputs.

Let us now consider some of the performance characteristics of DTSS. First of all, the dual processor system is capable of some 10 million multiplications per minute. Of course, not all of this is available to the users. With a load of 100 users, approximately 40 percent of the total available computing time is devoted to user jobs, 25 percent is needed for a variety of executive services, and the other 35 percent is "idle." These statistics need some explanation.

The idle time may under some circumstances be due to the fact that there are not enough users to keep the system busy. However, under a heavy load the explanation is quite different. Only a small fraction of the active jobs can be in high-speed memory ("in core") at any given time. Therefore, even with the best of scheduling algorithms, it will be quite common for all of the jobs in the high-speed core to have terminated or to be waiting for the result of some input/output operation (such as reading information from bulk memory). The existence of this idle time has been used as a criticism of time-sharing systems. However, in our experience it is outweighed by the great savings that can be accomplished in an interactive computer system. Not only are there great psychological advantages in being able to sit at the computer until your job is done, but there are significant savings in computer time. While a typical user is debugging his program in a batch-processing system, he will often request lengthy printouts of the memory contents in order to analyze his errors. In a batch-processing system these are all logged as useful computing time, while such complete printouts are never used in a time-sharing system. Since the user knows that he can make several requests in a minute, he will ask for a minimum amount of information in order to find his errors, and therefore debugging requires far less computer time in time sharing than in batch processing. I am thoroughly convinced that in computer usage time sharing is just as efficient as batch processing and certainly it is vastly more convenient and pleasant for human beings to use.

The 25 percent of computing time logged as executive services includes a wide variety of different tasks. Among these are all communications with the user, the scheduling of jobs, the moving of jobs from high-speed to bulk memory and back, and many other tasks that are in effect system overhead. However, the executive services also include many tasks which are specifically performed for the user but are too difficult to charge directly to him. Most notable among these are the analysis of user commands, the obtaining of various system functions for the user, and the carrying out of all kinds of editorial services. For example, if a user types in several corrections, the executive system must obtain a copy of his old program and make a variety of deletions, insertions, and corrections. Since this is accomplished at high speed by a single executive module, it is counted as an executive service.

Finally, 40 percent of the processing time is directly used by the customers. Since this amounts to the equivalent of 4 million multiplications a minute, even with

100 users on the system each has available to him computing power equal to 40,000 multiplications a minute. As we know from experience, this is ample for most users.

Let us next turn to the question of the bulk memory. Until about two years ago DTSS had only 20 million words of bulk memory and was continually running out of free space. It now has 72 million words, and even though system usage has expanded considerably, all indications are that this memory is sufficient.

Nearly 30 million words are reserved for copies of all systems programs, for the library programs, for the user catalogs, and for large data bases. That leaves more than 40 million words for user programs. In a given year more than 14,000 different people use DTSS. While we do not have an exact figure on the number of different users who have saved programs at any given time, 8,000 is a reasonable estimate. This would give the average user 5,000 words of bulk storage, which is much more than the vast majority of users need. The typical undergraduate student is restricted to 2,000 words of memory, and most students are never even aware of this limitation. In that space they can save half-a-dozen fair-sized programs, which is as many as most students ever want to have available at a given time.

A few further statistics may be of interest. For example, although a variety of languages, including FORTRAN, ALGOL, and COBOL, are available to all DTSS users, 98 percent of all programs, including most programs written by experts, are in BASIC. On a particularly busy day the system had an average of 100 simultaneous users during the busiest period in the afternoon, an average of 86 for the entire period from 8:00 a.m. to 1:00 a.m. and a peak of 111 users. On that day the system completed one user job every three seconds, for a total of 19,503 jobs for the day. Very few batch-processing systems could come close to that kind of record. Although more than 1,000 of the jobs required substantial computing time (ten seconds or more) the large total could be handled because 78 percent of the jobs required a second or less. Three-quarters of the users required a half hour or less at their terminals, and during that time they required less than four seconds of central processor time. The executive system carried out about one command per second, most of which fell into the following categories, given in order of importance:

1. Execute the program
2. Create a new program or retrieve an old one
3. Save a program
4. Give me a listing of my program
5. Perform an editorial function

On that very busy day new customers "signed on" 3197 times.

Evaluation

Time sharing has potentially brought the use of computers to millions of people. At the present time, time-sharing systems are still limited to educational institutions and fairly large businesses. But within those institutions anyone who is willing to take the trouble to learn a simple computer language now has access at first hand to the computer. Private computer service is still quite expensive, in part because progress in computer terminals has not kept up with progress in computers. But anyone can acquire a private terminal in his home, and an hour of terminal time a day, at the cost of maintaining a luxury car. Within the next two decades the price will undoubtedly come down to a level which will make computer terminals in the home quite common.

More importantly, the use of computers has been

made so simple that acquiring programming skill is no harder than learning how to use a large library. We can expect that in the next generation college graduates will have routinely learned how to make use of a high-speed computer. This is likely to have a revolutionary effect on the way human beings attack intellectual tasks. Some of the implications are discussed in later chapters.

And finally, time sharing provides a new dimension to computing: man and computer can now communicate directly and work as a team. We have only begun to use the new power that this provides for mankind. It will take another generation of both species to realize the full advantages of the new symbiosis.

4
Division of Labor

A Computer's Eye View

In the preceding chapter time sharing was examined from the point of view of human beings. It will help provide a different perspective on time sharing to examine it from the point of view of the computer. Since people have great difficulty in adjusting their minds to the incredible speed of the computer, I shall provide an analogy.

Let us suppose that space travelers discover a higher order of living beings. These creatures are much more intelligent than men, but their metabolism is much slower. We recognize their deep insights into problems and hope that they will help us to resolve a number of issues currently beyond human capability. On the other hand, they are so frustratingly slow that they must rely on our much faster response time in order to get the job done.

Specifically, I will assume that the amount of routine mental work (for example, computation) that a man can do in an hour will take these creatures a hundred years. They marvel at our great speed in carrying out calculations and yet they look down on us as a lower order of intelligence, whose strength lies in routine tasks, but which lacks their fundamental insights.

Suppose that a man goes to work for such a creature, hoping to combine the creature's higher intelligence with man's much greater speed. The relationship is quite frustrating. First of all, the creature takes two years to formulate the problem for his human companion. Man promptly goes to work and carries out the required calculations and arguments in a couple of weeks. When he presents his results to the creature, he must again wait months or years until the creature has absorbed these results and is ready to make a further suggestion. Needless to say, the human worker feels that his talents are wasted. He therefore offers his services to an entire tribe of creatures and finds that he can keep up with the requests of one hundred of them.

I will make the following assumptions about the various times involved in this analogy: The creature takes from three months to five years to get ready to enter a new request. The exact time may depend on how useful he finds the human results and how deeply he wants to think about the next step. Let us say that the average "turnaround time" is two years. The task is such that it may take anywhere from one day to a month of human effort, and I will assume that on the average it takes a week. Under these assumptions the human being can give good service to one hundred of the higher-order creatures.

The strategy will be as follows. He will work on a given job for a few days to see whether it can be quickly solved. If it can, he reports his results and turns to the next task. If he has failed to complete the job in—let us say—five days, he will set his calculations aside for awhile and work on some other creature's request. It is not efficient for him to work on each job until it is completed, because he may need to put in thirty days on a difficult task while the next task could have been completed in a single day. Since his main motivation is to give excellent service to his employers, he will try to complete short jobs as quickly as possible. It is not unreasonable for a creature that needs a full month of calculation to wait longer for the results, but one who needs only a day's computation expects his answers in a hurry.

I have tried out such a system on the computer (in a

mode known as "simulation," which is discussed in Chapter 11), and it appears that the human being would be able to give excellent service to all 100 employers. I simulated the behavior of this human-creature system over a period of twenty years. On the average each creature has to wait two months for his results. Since he then takes from several months to several years to decide what to do with the results, this will seem like very fast service. In twenty years creatures can on the average have nine to ten jobs completed by their human servants. Since they take two years on the average to decide what to do next, it is clear that the service cannot be improved very much. Each creature will be spending more than 90 percent of the time thinking about what he wants done and less than 10 percent waiting for the next result. This is a highly satisfactory working relationship.

The human being is kept busy all or most of the time. Occasionally a fairly long backlog of several months' work will build up, but typically he will have only a half dozen jobs to worry about at a given time. This is due to the fact that, from the human point of view, these intelligent creatures are so very slow in making up their minds about what they want next. In five different attempts to simulate the twenty-year period, I found that the human being in the best case caught up with all his work at the end of twenty years while in the worst case he had eleven jobs pending with a backlog of three and a half months. The slowest of the creatures had only four jobs completed in twenty years, while some who seemed to respond rapidly to human results succeeded in completing seventeen jobs, which is superbly fast action on the time scale of these slow creatures.

If the reader will now substitute computers for human beings, human beings for the more intelligent creatures, and reduce the time scale by a million, he will understand the computers' point of view about time sharing.

The Problem of Communication

Let us follow the analogy further by asking how the two species should communicate with each other. First of all, it is clear that for human beings to learn the language of the slow but intelligent creatures is more efficient than the reverse process. Even given the greater intelligence of the creatures, it would take each one several hundred years to learn the language of human beings. On the other hand, a human being can be expected to learn the rudiments of a new language in a month. While it may be that the greater subtleties and finer overtones of the creature's language are beyond the understanding of human beings, a rudimentary version of the language will suffice for collaboration. This is precisely what we do when we teach a language like BASIC to the computer.

However, the real difficulty in communication does not come in the choice of a language but in the decision of how frequently computers should report to human beings and just which of their results we should see. Let us return to our analogy to explore this problem.

Our creatures cannot monitor a human servant's work in any detail, because it would take them forever to absorb what looks to them like vast amounts of calculations. Instead, they send a task to a human being and tell him that when he has reached a certain point he should report the most interesting features of his results. Their dilemma is that if they asked a human being to report too often, they would take months or years to absorb the results and thus significantly delay the work. On the other hand, if they let the human being go too far without reporting to them, they run the risk that they will have wasted a good deal of his efforts, since at an earlier stage, through insight, they could have put him on a more fruitful path. The creatures often express their frustration by saying that if only human beings were truly intelligent they could evaluate their own work all along the way and save the creatures a great deal of trouble. And man can reply, with some justice, that if he had the deep insight of the more intelligent creatures then he would have no need for their collaborative help.

A second dilemma faces the creatures in deciding just how much detail the human being should present to them. If results are presented in very great detail, it will take the creatures many years to absorb them. On the other hand, if they ask for only a small number of salient features, they run the risk of throwing away a result that would have been most useful to them.

The chances are that the creatures will adopt a trial-and-error method. They take a guess as to how often the human being should report and what the most important results may be. If the work is proceeding more slowly than they expect, they may next time ask the human being to work a few days longer before he reports his next results. If they feel that he has taken an incorrect turn, they will ask him to redo his work and report more frequently. Similar trial-and-error methods will be adopted for the amount of detail that is reported. Again it may be necessary to redo some work and report more of the details.

The dilemmas here attributed to the creatures are precisely the dilemmas that face human beings in working with the computer. If we monitor the work of the computer at fairly frequent intervals, we slow it down considerably. If we monitor it too infrequently we may find that half the work it did was totally useless. If we ask it to print out only a half dozen of the most interesting quantities computed, we may overlook an unexpected factor that would influence our thinking. If we ask it to print out its result in tremendous detail, we are faced with the task of scanning many pages of printed output, which is wasteful and inefficient for human beings. Therefore, we adopt a trial-and-error procedure in which we do not hesitate to have the computer go back and redo a calculation, showing more details.

The temptation, of course, is to try to teach the computer how to evaluate its own results more intelligently. We would love to be able to tell it to go on and work as long as necessary and not to bother us until something interesting turns up. As soon as it finds something interesting it is to let us know. The only catch in this very promising recipe is the necessity of explaining to the computer just when a result is interesting.

A great deal of work has gone on, under the general title of "artificial intelligence," to try to teach a higher form of intelligence to computers. The decade of the 1960s showed that this task is vastly more difficult than some of the proponents of artificial intelligence had guessed. Although there have been a number of notable successes, in many cases the human effort to teach the computer has turned out to be horrendous, and the amount of labor required for a computer to simulate human intelligence is discouragingly great. Often it reaches a point at which the effort is simply not worthwhile.

For example, various groups have taught the computer to do simple manipulation of mathematical formulas, let us say at the level of freshman calculus. While it is entirely possible to do this, it is not uncommon to find that even after a tremendous human teaching effort the computer performs these tasks no faster than a human being does. When one considers the computers' great advantage in speed, it is clear that the computer must somehow be doing these tasks "the wrong way." The irony is that the tasks that freshmen calculus students find most difficult, such as learning the basic rules of differentiation (particularly the chain rule), are very simple for computers, while other tasks that are trivial for human beings seem to be very difficult for computers. It is notable that very often a computer takes much longer to simplify its answer than to obtain the answer in the first place. We have not yet found a computer counterpart of the human being's ability to "just look at the formula and note certain simplifications."

Whether we consider the analogy with the creatures or an actual man-computer relation, it is clear that it is always the responsibility of the higher intelligence to make the judgments. If the results turn out wrong the fault is the master's, not the servant's. After all, the creatures understand the strength and limitations of human beings, but the reverse is not true. Therefore, the creatures must plan a procedure for solving a problem and give absolutely clear instructions as to how the human servant should carry out his task. The creatures will try to formulate instructions in such a way that the human being can clearly recognize when he has reached the goal. As a safeguard the creatures must also tell the human being to watch out for certain types of errors that may crop up in the work. Since they can never be absolutely sure that their proposed procedure will work, they will also put a time limit on the human being, probably several times that which they estimate as necessary to solve the problem. If their human servant has not succeeded in completing the problem in the allowed time, the chances are that something has gone wrong with the computation and more intelligent creatures will have to look at his results.

Guidelines

I hope that the reader has not found the previous section totally satisfactory. I do not find it satisfactory myself. One would like to have much clearer guidelines as to how man and machine should collaborate. These do not exist today. There is, it seems to me, a great need for more experts to carry on intensive research on the best means of collaboration between man and computer.

However, a few "dos" and "don'ts" can help. For example, it makes no sense for a human being to carry out a task which a computer can do equally easily in a fraction of the time. A good example of this is the rule that, in a modern time-sharing system, it is unnecessary to print out hundreds of pages of output (a procedure that used to be quite common under batch processing). After all, what can a human being do with these hundreds of pages except to scan them mechanically for a few interesting conclusions? It would have been much simpler to instruct the computer itself to scan these pages and report only a summary to the human being.

On the other hand, it makes no sense for human beings to spend several days teaching a computer a task that a human being could do himself in an hour. In the present state of the art most of the attempts to teach higher intelligence to computers come under this heading. However, this rule has a clear-cut exception: if there is a task that human beings have to carry out over and over again, it may well be worthwhile instead to spend several days teaching a computer how to do it. It is also worthwhile to invest considerable effort in developing "artificial intelligence" in computers in the hope of possible future payoffs.

An important guideline in writing computer programs is the rule that one must think out ahead of time what results one expects to obtain from the computer and what computer results need to be printed to help in reaching a conclusion. The first violation of this rule, which I mentioned earlier, is by the programmer who writes a long program which requires a great deal of computation but forgets to instruct the computer to print the answer. This may sound ludicrous, but it has happened to every user of computers. An even more common error is to ask for a small number of results only to find that additional figures are needed. This usually means that the computer has to duplicate its entire work. Whether the output will be too small or too great depends on the type of problem. But this dilemma deserves a great deal of further research.

Next we must face the fact that if we ask a computer to carry out several million calculations there is a very strong probability that something will go wrong. Therefore, we must build a number of checks into the program to spot troubles as soon as they occur. Without these checks, we would know only that the final answers are total nonsense, with no clue whatsoever as to what went wrong. While no checks are ever foolproof, if enough of them are provided, the answers that come out have a high probability of being those desired. The difficulty here is that it is extremely difficult for any human being to anticipate all the things that can go wrong in several million calculations.

Modern computer languages have a number of such checks built into them. This means simply that one of the rules under which the computer proceeds is that the user will automatically be informed if certain catastrophes occur. For example, the computer will warn the user if it has been told to take the square root of a negative number. You may wonder why a human being would ever tell a computer to do this, but that question overlooks the fundamental difficulty of communication. In a given program, at some point, perhaps after the completion of a million calculations, the computer is asked to take the square root of a number which was designated as x. The catch is that it took the computer a million steps to find out the value of x, and at the beginning the programmer had no idea what it was going to turn out to be. Presumably, if the computer was asked to take the square root of x, the programmer had assumed that x would be positive. Therefore, if after a million calculations x proves to be negative, it is well that the computer promptly notifies the user and stops, because the chances are that something has gone drastically wrong.

This is a simple and obvious example. The trouble with communication with computers is the fact that so far we have been able to teach computers how to make only the simplest of judgments. We wish that computers would let us know when we are getting close to a solution or when we seem to be getting nowhere at all. We wish that they could explore thousands of different patterns and pick out the interesting ones. We wish that they could spot errors in logic as well as errors in the syntax of the instructions. In short, we wish that computers were more intelligent. But perhaps this is the burden that we more intelligent creatures have to bear, and perhaps it is a comfort that our very slow progress in imparting intelligence to computers assures us that human beings are not going to become obsolete too fast.

5
Symbiote or Parasite?

The Popular Reaction to Computers

Most people would concede that computers are strange new entities that have a significant impact on human life. However, I would suspect that most of them would classify the species of computer as a harmful partner rather than as a symbiote. Why has popular reaction to computers been so negative?

First of all, computers are convenient scapegoats. My sister tells the story of going into a department store on Long Island at which she has shopped for many years. She asked the salesgirl whether a certain item was in stock and was told that she could not answer that question because that information was kept by a computer. My sister is sufficiently sophisticated about computers to know that they are supposed to make more information available rather than less. She also points out that this same salesgirl had never previously been able to answer any question as to which items were in stock; therefore, she suspects that the salesgirl is delighted to have computers to blame for her ignorance.

A much deeper-lying human fear about computers may be summarized by the common complaint: "We are all being turned into numbers." I consider this a legitimate complaint. Actually the problem is due not to the existence of computers but to the fact that early computer usage was most unsophisticated. If you wish to keep track of a million human beings (for example, customers in a store or citizens in a city), it is much more efficient to code them numerically than to try to search by name. Our method of naming people has great redundancies and inefficiencies built into it. It is quite common for two people to have the same name. It is very easy to misspell a long name. Furthermore, people do not always write their name the same way. Sometimes they will use a full middle name and sometimes only a middle initial, sometimes only a first name, at other times a nickname, and so on. It is therefore perfectly reasonable for internal purposes to assign a number to each human being. But it is most unreasonable to expect a human being to memorize that number.

Indeed, the difficulty here is exactly analogous to that originally faced with computer languages. Until we realized how simple it was to teach a computer a language easily understandable to human beings, we forced all human users to learn a horrible computer language. With modern computers it would be perfectly simple to ask the computer to recognize the human being's name and find his code number, instead of forcing millions of human beings to use numbers in place of their names. For example, on a push-button telephone it should be entirely possible to "type in" a party's name and rough address and have the telephone company computer find his phone number and dial it. Of course this will mean extra use of a computer, and therefore an extra charge should be made for the service, just as person-to-person calls are made at a premium.

In short, I believe that the number syndrome is a legitimate human complaint, but with more intelligent use of computers the trend can be reversed.

Next there is the common human fear that massive computers will be "Big Brother watching us." Indeed, there are a number of deep legal and moral questions concerning invasion of privacy, but I will not attempt to discuss these in this book.[1] It is important to remember, however, that computers do only what they are told to do. If governments and big businesses are allowed to invade our privacy, it is our own fault for allowing them to do so. They are perfectly capable of doing this without computers, although computers make it much easier to keep track of millions of people. Computers have lowered the price tag for Big Brother but have not brought about a change in principle. Questions such as whether we have the right to see what information governments or finance companies have on us, and whether we have a right to correct erroneous information, must be answered. But this is a problem to be solved by legal experts, not by computer experts.

The Deeper Problems

Let us suppose that stores become enlightened enough to forbid their employees to blame their own shortcomings on computers. Let us suppose that computers are taught to call us by our names rather than by numbers, and that people can be truthfully assured that sufficient legal safeguards have been implemented on large data files. Let us also suppose that we no longer receive communications on IBM cards that are not to be folded or mutilated and that all other obvious annoyances are removed. There would remain two fundamental complaints of human beings which would require massive efforts to correct.

Modern computers were invented to solve highly complex scientific problems. It was an accidental benefit, only slowly recognized by business, that the very same computers were incredibly efficient bookkeeping machines. Then the drive was on to employ computers to increase productivity, to cut down costs, and to produce greater efficiency. Companies had great hopes that computers could replace hundreds of employees. Needless to say, this did not make computers popular with employees. Fortunately, it has rarely been the case that computerization has reduced the existing staff; it is much more common that along with computers exactly the same staff is needed but the staff can perform better and accomplish more. (I will ignore examples where more people are accomplishing less.) But almost all the applications of computers in the first two decades were designed to improve the operation of the corporation and not to make life pleasanter for the customers. Only very recently have companies begun to realize that at very modest additional computer expense they can give vastly better service.

I would like to see a fundamental change in philosophy on the part of both government and business. Both should be willing to spend more to make life better and easier for everyone. Indeed, this will be a major theme throughout the remainder of this book. Only when such a philosophy is adopted generally can we look forward to a time when the average human being will look at the computer as a friend rather than a foe.

The second and even more fundamental reason that human beings generally dislike computers is, I believe, the fact that they tend to approach modern high-speed computers with a peculiar combination of fear and awe. The source of this reaction is ignorance.

Most people today grew up when no modern computers were in existence. While the same situation applied to automobiles in the early twentieth century, a fairly rapid change took place. Even if not everyone drove an automobile, almost everyone had a friend who owned one. Automobiles quickly became common on our streets, and their principles of operation were simple and easily understood. Unfortunately, the average person does not have the foggiest idea of just what a computer is or how it works. And, since computers are shielded from them by the high priests of the profession, all their acquaintance is from a distance.

Human beings automatically fear anything strange that they don't understand. They have an almost superstitious attitude toward computers, to which they attribute both too much and too little. They cannot really comprehend that computers can do millions of routine tasks in a minute. Therefore it looks miraculous to them that a computer can do all the calculations in a complicated income-tax return in a fraction of a second. On the other hand, they tend to attribute too much intelligence to computers, to the point where any nonsensical answer will be accepted if they are told that the work was done by a computer.

I have heard a story about the design of a new freeway in the City of Los Angeles. At an open hearing a number of voters complained bitterly that the freeway would go right through the midst of a part of the city heavily populated by blacks and would destroy the spirit of community that they had slowly and painfully built up. The voters' arguments were defeated by the simple statement that, according to an excellent computer, the proposed route was the best possible one. Apparently none of them knew enough to ask how the computer had been instructed to evaluate the variety of possible routes. Was it asked only to consider costs of building and acquisition of property (in which case it would have found routing through a ghetto area highly advantageous), or was it also asked to take into account the amount of human suffering that a given route would cause? Perhaps the voters would even have agreed that it is not possible to measure human suffering in terms of dollars. But if we omit consideration of human suffering, then we are equating its cost to zero, which is certainly the worst of all procedures!

Therefore I conclude that to change people's attitude toward computers will require a massive educational effort. Until we can bring up a new generation of human beings who are thoroughly acquainted with the power and limitations of computers, who know what questions have to be asked and answered, and who are not intimidated by computer experts in a debate, we cannot hope for a fundamental change. I see great promise in the reactions of recent Dartmouth students. Now that most of them have first-hand experience with computers, they approach computer applications without fear or superstition and with considerable understanding of how computers can serve mankind.

Will the species of computers turn out to be a parasite or a symbiote? I would argue that the answer to that question is entirely up to man. He is the dominant partner in the relationship. If human beings collectively have enough understanding and enough foresight, they can assure that the interaction between the two species will be totally beneficial to mankind.

Part Two

Symbiotic Evolution

6
A Look at the Future

More Power to the Computer

Within one generation we have witnessed fantastic growth in the power of the computer. It is therefore reasonable to ask what we can expect in the next generation.

It sounds plausible to say that since computing speed has been increased by a factor of a million in twenty-five years a similar increase in speed can be expected in the next twenty-five. However, this brings us up against one of the absolute limitations in nature—uamely, the speed of light.

Consider a computer that ran 1000 times as fast as current computers—that is, its basic cycle time was a nanosecond (one-billionth of a second). While we tend to think that signals traveling at the speed of light arrive instantaneously, we know that this is actually not so. It is true that telephone communications between any two points on earth do not involve noticeable delays, but anyone who watched communications with astronauts on the moon knows that it takes more than a second for a radio signal to reach the moon. Therefore, the speed of light becomes important when distances are astronomical or when the time span becomes very short.

SPEED OF LIGHT

Second	186,000 miles
Millisecond	186 miles
Microsecond	980 feet
Nanosecond	1 foot

Light travels one foot in a nanosecond. Therefore a computer that is to have a basic cycle time of one nanosecond must be able to send the signal from any point in the machine to any other point without traveling more than a foot. This requires a highly miniaturized computer. While such a miniaturized machine is entirely conceivable, it will be expensive and will certainly represent the outer limits of what we can achieve in the way of improvement of speed.

There are certain special computers now on the market that operate at better than microsecond speed, but these are usually computers that do "parallel processing"—that is, they basically operate at the microsecond speed but can do many, say 100, operations simultaneously. Whether this trick has economic advantages over having a hundred separate computers depends entirely on the kind of task one wishes to undertake. For most ordinary uses this is probably the wrong way to construct computers. However, for certain "real time" jobs, when calculations must be completed within a fixed amount of time, parallel processors are the answer.

It is therefore safe to assume that, while future computers will be somewhat faster than those of today, the increase in speed will not be nearly as spectacular as it was in the recent past. However, there are several other areas in which we can look forward to continuing spectacular improvements.

Miniaturization and new technology such as laser beams can make computer memories vastly larger even than the large memories of today. As I have mentioned, computer memories that will hold the entire *Encyclopaedia Britannica* are commonly in use today. But memories a thousand times that large have appeared on the market. I fully expect that within the next generation we will see computer memories capable of holding the contents of the largest library in the world.

COMPUTER MEMORY CAPACITIES

1945	10 words
1955	Small book
1965	Set of encyclopaedia
1975	Million-volume library

One can increase the power of a given computer system by duplicating its parts. Indeed, DTSS operates with four separate computers (two for processing and two for communications) with one of the four serving as a master. Once one has solved the problems of programming several cooperating computers, there is very little difficulty extending the programs to a computer system which would have twenty or thirty processors. The addition of one more processor or one more communications computer is a trivial task on DTSS.

The same question arises here that I have already raised about parallel processing: Is it better to have several computers work as part of a single system, or to have them work as separate computer systems? There is always a certain overhead involved in the communication among computers. But when several computers are part of a single integrated system, the load can be divided more equitably and all of the computers can have access to the same memory and the same peripherals. For example, Dartmouth's card-handling equipment, printer, and tapes are used nowhere nearly to capacity, and therefore additional processors could be added without having to duplicate these peripherals. The addition of more processors (and hence more users) would require an increase in the memory of the computer, but it would still be more efficient than splitting the computing center into two. In the latter case, each user would insist on calling into the part of the center that contained his program, and the users would have to be arbitrarily divided into two categories which could not communicate with each other. In addition, all programs, such as library programs and systems software, that are common to all users would have to be duplicated.

While we have witnessed remarkable reductions in cost per computation in the last generation, I expect to see further spectacular improvements. In the last few years entirely new techniques have been developed for the inexpensive production of electronic circuitry, such as printed circuits. These will enable manufacturers to produce computers with today's capacities at a fraction of the present cost. The same is true for memories, since the much larger memories I mentioned are only slightly more expensive than those of today.

The one area that is lagging behind the rest in cost improvement is the very important one of computer terminals. A cost of $100 per month is quite typical for the rental and servicing of a computer terminal. And these terminals are fairly primitive; more attractive terminals are even more expensive. I see absolutely no reason why a very reliable computer terminal could not be manufactured to sell for the price of a black-and-white television set. This will be necessary if computers are to be brought into the home.

I have discussed the possibilities of modest increases in speed, spectacular increases in memory capacity, the ability to put together much larger and more powerful computer systems, and major savings in cost. But the next single most important development is likely to be the effective combination of computers and the communications network.

Computers and Communications

The telephone was a lovely toy when it was first invented; it was great fun to talk to somebody next door. It did not become a major factor in modern civilization until it was tied into a national and eventually into an international communications network. Fortunately, such a network now exists, and modern technology makes it possible to expand its capacity significantly. Coaxial cables, microwave links, and communications satellites give it an additional dimension.

The next decade is likely to see the development of huge computer networks. Indeed several modest networks are in existence today, such as the airline reservation system, General Electric's time-sharing network, and the Western Union computer network. As I mentioned in Chapter 3, DTSS was once demonstrated in Scotland, which shows that computer communication at distances of thousands of miles presents no problem. The full impact of modern computers will be felt by most people only when large multiprocessor computer centers are built all over the United States and tied efficiently into the existing communications network.

Once one or more general-purpose national networks exist, entirely new capabilities can be added to computers. For example, a large company that has branches all over the country can keep its information in the network and have access to it from any branch office. An educational program can be inserted anywhere in the network and be easily available to 90 percent of the population by means of a local call. If a collection of standard programs can be made available economically, this would take care of the commonest tasks for which most people need computers. One could dial in, explain the problem, and have the appropriate program found in the computer's library. Such a network would indeed be a major breakthrough in business, education, research, and many other areas. Let us consider how such a network might be built.

Building a Network

How difficult would it be to build a computer network in the United States? Here I discuss this in terms of computers; in Chapter 8 I will also consider it in relation to a national automated library.

It would be desirable to design the network in such a way that most users could reach it through a local telephone call. A good initial target would be the eighty cities which had populations of 150,000 or more in the 1960 census. Computer centers could be placed in strategic locations all over the country and relay stations added in each of these cities. These cities in themselves represent only about a quarter of the population of the nation, but if all their suburbs are included, plus smaller cities that can be picked up "on the way," the United States would be blanketed fairly thoroughly.

For the location of the computer centers, I considered key cities with fairly large populations so located that practically all of the eighty target cities would be within 500 miles of one of the centers. In calculating distance I used road mileages, since telephone lines generally follow roads. With more modern techniques, such as microwave relays, it would be possible to shorten these distances. A little experimenting indicated that seven centers would do the job adequately: at New York, Chicago, Atlanta, Dallas, Los Angeles, Denver, and Seattle.

Only two of the eighty target cities, Miami and El Paso, are more than 520 miles from one of these centers. The average customer is 177 miles from the nearest center. Note that this is quite different from the question of how far the average city is from a center, since the strategic choice of centers assures that the huge populations of New York, Chicago, and Los Angeles are right at a center. When one looks at the distribution of load among the seven centers, one finds that Denver and Seattle carry a very small portion of the total. Nevertheless these locations are necessary for good geographic distribution. These cities and their customers might be accommodated by having major relay stations rather than actual centers in Denver and Seattle. A cost-effectiveness calculation is needed to determine whether this would reduce the total cost.

Next one finds that Chicago and New York would carry too heavy a burden. It is economically reasonable to relieve the load on these two cities by putting additional centers in Cleveland and Baltimore. If this is done, the average customer will be only 142 miles from a center. This is considerably less than the maximum distance from Dartmouth College to its farthest user, and a perfectly practical figure to use for planning purposes. The distribution of load now looks as follows:

Center	Cities Served	Percent of Load
Atlanta	11	7.8
Baltimore	5	9.4
Chicago	13	17.7
Cleveland	12	13.9
Dallas	13	10.8
Denver	3	2.0
Los Angeles	9	12.6
New York	11	23.3
Seattle	3	2.5
Total	80	100.0

This distribution is not necessarily optimal, but it is at least fairly close to being so, and it shows that nine computation centers, strategically placed, can serve the whole country efficiently.

Further efficiency can be built into the system by tying the nine centers together by high-speed telephone lines or microwave links. In this way one center can substitute for another in case of catastrophe and also handle an overload on a sister installation. This load-sharing technique is now in use in the United States to take care of the differences in time zones. Since New Yorkers arrive at work three hours earlier than people in California, a West Coast station can carry some of the eastern load in the early hours of the morning. In return, eastern stations can help out the West Coast late in the afternoon. The staggered hours for lunch in various parts of the country can be similarly handled. Nevertheless, there will be certain peak periods at which a given system would be overloaded. However, techniques exist for smoothing out such a load.

On DTSS there is an important service available known as "background." For certain long-running jobs the user types in a request for background operation and then leaves his terminal. His job is carried out whenever the computer has some spare time and the results will be available to him minutes or hours later, depending on the load. By having such background service available at all the centers at reduced rates, it is possible to adjust peak-hour loads.

Finally, each center could control its load by regulating the number of telephone lines it makes available to its customers. Suppose it is estimated that a center can handle 1000 telephone lines with an average distribution of requests. As a safety margin it will probably make 1200 lines available. If there are 1000 customers on the system and spare capacity still seems to be available, it will allow additional customers to come on. However, if the computer complex finds that with only 800 customers it is already heavily loaded, it will turn the remaining telephone lines to "busy" status so that no new customers can come on until the load decreases. A beneficial effect of this device is the fact that customers soon learn what the hours are when they are likely to get busy signals and, whenever it is convenient, will arrange to come on the system when it is less heavily loaded.

Evolution

What I have just been describing is the predictable evolution of the computer species. We expect to see individual computers that are somewhat faster, have much greater memories, and are more compact. But the multi-computer systems and the computer networks are likely to be the most important evolutionary developments.

I am reminded of those science fiction stories in which man meets a strange species that has communal consciousness. The creatures share memories, can monitor one another's thought processes and work on problems as a community. It is my contention that such fiction is about to become reality. We are witnessing even now the evolution of a species in which the individual is subsumed under a group consciousness. Indeed it is a telepathic race. And I expect that computer networks will display all the marvelous traits that science fiction predicted for such strange beings.

My major concern is whether man can keep up with his symbiotic partner. Even today computers have more power than we know how to use. We can keep the machines busy, but many computer experts feel that we have not yet learned how to make full use of their capabilities. Therefore a rapid social and scientific evolution must take place if man is to maintain the role of a full partner. This, I predict, is one of the most exciting challenges facing mankind.

7
Computers in Education

First Attempts

Much of the early interaction between human beings and computers occurred in the field of education. I believe that education will continue to be one of the important areas for computer applications—in spite of the fact that we witnessed a false start.

Throughout the 1960s far-reaching claims were made for the potential for computers to improve education. The efforts, particularly of computer companies, were concentrated on "Computer-Aided Instruction" or "CAI." While the phrase computer-aided instruction is broad enough to describe all current applications of computers to the process of education, in practice CAI has come to stand for only one possible use of the computer —namely, as a substitute teacher.[1]

Students sitting at computer terminals can receive instruction in a wide variety of subjects. A perennial favorite is language instruction. This can consist of vocabulary, grammar, and spelling drills, or of monitored language translation in a more sophisticated version. For example, the computer may provide words in English, for which the student is supposed to give synonyms in French.

Similar drill problems can be provided in many topics in arithmetic. I myself once used a home terminal to drill my son on the addition of fractions. The computer would randomly pick two not very complicated fractions and ask my son to type in the sum and to simplify it. The computer would either approve the answer, tell him that the answer was incorrect, or tell him that it was correct but not in simplest form. It also kept score for him and gave him a grade at the end of a series of problems. Although this is the most simple-minded drill program, two afternoons spent with the computer helped my son overcome a psychological block about the addition of fractions.

In a more sophisticated application CAI will teach the student new subject matter and quiz him on it. Textual material is provided either directly on a display terminal or through supplementary notes. When the student feels that he has mastered a topic, the computer will quiz him and allow him to proceed only if it is satisfied that the student has really understood the major ideas in the section.

A major claim made for CAI is that each student can proceed at his own speed. Since the subject matter is presented by means of a computer program, it is possible to build a great deal of sophistication into the instructions to achieve this variable speed. A large number of questions are provided to test each idea. The student who is able to answer several questions correctly is immediately allowed to proceed to the next topic without completing the entire series of exercises. An average student would complete all the exercises and then go on to the next section. The student who is having difficulty with a given topic, as shown through the number of errors he commits, can branch out to another program and be provided with remedial instructional material. In this sense CAI is more individualized than the instruction the average teacher can provide to a class.

The computer also has certain attributes which in special situations makes it superior to the teacher. First, the computer has infinite patience. If it is necessary to provide the student with a hundred exercises of the same type, the computer will proceed to do so, read all the answers carefully, and provide appropriate comments. Second, through time sharing, it can simultaneously drill a large number of students, each one proceeding at his or her own speed. Third, the computer, if correctly programmed, does not make any mistakes. And, finally, there are distinct advantages in the completely impersonal relation between the student and the computer. The student can make all his mistakes in private without having to demonstrate his ignorance to the teacher and to the rest of the class. All these advantages have to be acknowledged.

Several years ago there was a considerable drive to sell special-purpose devices for CAI. As has happened several times in the brief history of modern computers, the special-purpose machines could not compete with today's general-purpose computers. A large and fast general-purpose computer, operating as a time-sharing system, provides vastly more flexibility and leaves the instructor maximum freedom. Instead of having to modify the hardware for each different instructional mode, he can write his programs according to his own best understanding of the pedagogical needs. Given such a large time-sharing system CAI will be as good as the instructor's program can make it.

Shortcomings of CAI

I have, however, two major prejudices against CAI. These are, first, that the computer is a very expensive substitute for a book, and, second, that it is a very poor substitute for a teacher.

The only possible way that I can justify feeding pages of a book through a computer to a computer terminal is that the younger generation has been hypnotized by television and is willing to read only if the material appears on a screen. Even though an entire book can be stored conveniently and inexpensively in a computer memory, if the pages of a book are merely produced for the user exactly as they were typed in, nothing is gained. It would be faster, much cheaper, and just as convenient to have the user bring the textbook with him and turn to the appropriate page when instructed by the computer.

We are again suffering from the "all or nothing" syndrome. Just as in the early days of computers there was a tendency to assign tasks entirely to machines or entirely to human beings, early CAI attempts seemed to try to turn over as much of the work as possible to a computer. It is much more sensible to let students read a page, or better a chapter, of a book on their own and then go to the computer terminal to be drilled or tested.

My second major objection is based on the fact that there are very few CAI applications in which a computer can give the same quality of education that a human teacher can provide. I have mentioned a few distinct advantages of computers over human beings in teaching, but in most instances the disadvantages outweigh them. In writing a CAI program the instructor must anticipate every possible response to a long series of questions. The more freedom provided for a student in answering the questions, the harder it is to anticipate the responses. Therefore there is an almost irresistible temptation to strait-jacket the student.

CAI programs are most effective for rote learning and mechanical drill. This is why so many successes in vocabulary drills or in testing simple arithmetical skills are reported. In these cases the answers are unique or nearly unique. But even here there are situations where the handling of student responses is far from satisfactory. For example, a student who translates a foreign word as "teakup" will be told by the computer that this is an incorrect translation, while a human teacher would immediately recognize it as a correct translation incorrectly spelled. Since most schoolchildren are poor spellers and even poorer typists, CAI exercises can become frustrating.

These problems can be solved, in principle, by much more sophisticated programming that tries to recognize certain common misspellings or mistypings. Indeed, advocates of CAI generally concede that today's programs are far from satisfactory, but they believe that much better programs are on the horizon. I predict that writing really first-rate CAI programs will be vastly more difficult than most of its advocates now realize.

And even the most sophisticated CAI programs cannot anticipate what a truly creative student will do. There is a famous anecdote about the German mathematician Karl Friederich Gauss (1777–1855) who was probably the greatest mathematician of all time. When he was a young child, he seems to have always pestered his teacher for more challenging arithmetical problems. Therefore one day the teacher greeted him at the door with a long piece of paper on which the numbers from 1 to 100 had been written and told him to spend the class period adding up these numbers. The teacher had barely started the class when Gauss raised his hand and said, "5,050." The teacher asked, "What is 5,050?" and Gauss replied, "That is the answer." The teacher, infuriated, sat down and spent the rest of the class period adding up the numbers himself; he found that the answer was indeed 5,050. Of course Gauss had no intention of carrying out so boring an arithmetical task. He looked at the list for a minute and realized that 1 plus 100 equals 101, 2 plus 99 equals 101, and so on. Therefore, there were fifty pairs of numbers each adding up to 101, and 50 times 101 equals 5,050.

I once had a nightmare in which the young Gauss was back in school, but the school was being taught by a CAI computer system. In this system the computer told Gauss to take 1 and add 2 to it, then it forced him to add 3 to the result, and so on. By the time he had added the numbers to 100, he had become thoroughly disgusted with mathematics and decided to become a lawyer!

An Alternative Approach

At Dartmouth an enormous amount of computer-aided instruction takes place, but less than 1 percent of this is technically CAI. Instead, the computer is used as a powerful tool (for information retrieval and for lengthy calculations) and is also available to be taught by the students.

CAI uses only a small fraction of the capacity of a modern computer. The ability to carry on a conversation with many users is important, and so is the ability to program and to get almost instantaneous responses no matter which way the CAI program branches. However, little or no use is made of the computational powers of the computer and of its immense potential for information retrieval.

The opportunity to put a modern computer at the fingertips of all of the students has made the Dartmouth mathematics and science courses both more palatable and more meaningful. Students do not spend endless hours doing arithmetical calculations. Nor are they limited to the usual trivial kind of problems—such as what happens when one billiard ball hits another one. Instead, it is their job to grasp the principles taught in mathematics and science classes; all the messy arithmetic is left to the computers. We can also introduce any college student to meaningful practical applications of a theory that is taught in class. In a mechanics course, the only difference between significant applications and trivial ones is that the former may require many more computations.

In the social sciences it is the information retrieval potential of the computer that has made a vast difference. It is now possible to store several large data bases of some millions of pieces of data each. A user can extract in seconds the information necessary for his work and then has the computational power of the computer automatically available to carry out a variety of statistical tests. Project IMPRESS at Dartmouth is just such a system.

A Sociology 1 student can sit down at a terminal and request access to a large sample of the latest United States census. He can then indicate the variables he wishes to study; for example, age, sex, race, level of education, and level of income. A minute later he has available to him a summary table (technically known as a "cross-tab") on which he can perform a variety of statistical tests. For example, he can test whether in a given group of the same age, race, and educational level there are differences in income based on sex. (He would find that in each category men earn significantly more than women.)

SAMPLE OUTPUT FROM IMPRESS

Sex by School by Earning

PERCENT

	Low		Medium		High	
	MALE	FEMALE	MALE	FEMALE	MALE	FEMALE
Elementary	62.0	94.7	34.5	4.7	3.4	0.5
High school	47.9	90.1	47.1	9.4	4.9	0.4
College	32.4	74.8	47.5	23.1	20.0	1.9

The extraction and structuring of derived data from a huge data file will use up a minute of computing time, but statistical tables are constructed in a few seconds, and one can learn a great deal in a half-hour session.

The most spectacular educational impact of DTSS, however, was one not foreseen by the designers. Most of our students write a great many programs for the computer. In this process the student is the teacher and the computer is the student. The students learn an enormous amount by being forced to teach the computer how to solve a given problem. Much of the teaching of mathematics and science consists in the development of algorithms, or recipes, for the solution of problems. In traditional education, the student is supposed to absorb an algorithm by working out three examples of it. Quite typically the student gets so involved in the complexities of the arithmetic or algebra involved that he completely loses track of the algorithm itself. When he programs a computer to work out the examples, the exact opposite occurs. The student must concentrate on the basic principles; he must understand the algorithm thoroughly in order to be able to explain it to a computer. On the other hand, he does not have to do any of the arithmetic or algebra. At Dartmouth we have seen hundreds of examples of spectacular success of learning through teaching the computer.

What Is Needed

Let me summarize the present state of the use of computers in instruction. Although the original effort was concentrated entirely on CAI, and far-reaching claims were made for it, the success of CAI has been limited. Use of CAI is typically very expensive and is likely to remain so for a long time. While there are many types of legitimate CAI applications in areas of routine drill and rote learning, CAI is a very poor substitute for a teacher in the "higher" learning situations. On the other hand, a general-purpose computer in time-sharing mode provides more sophisticated uses of the computer in education, the most notable being the use of the arithmetical power of the machines to allow the student to calculate real-life applications; the use of the computer for large-scale information retrieval, usually coupled with statistical techniques; and the very important use by the student to teach the machine how to solve problems. These applications not only lead to more sophisticated learning situations but are much cheaper in use of computer and terminal time than CAI. In addition, since they clearly supplement classroom activity rather than replace it, they in no way threaten the job of the teacher.

There is another fundamental difference between the two types of uses. The kinds of applications common in DTSS teach the student how to program the computer in ways that take advantage of its full power and avoid its limitations. Most students leave Dartmouth with a thorough understanding of the nature of modern computers and with a good idea as to how they may be used in later life. Since in CAI the student plays a rather passive role, somewhat like learning a language from a phonograph record, none of these benefits accrue.

I consider it imperative for the benefit of mankind that during the next decade computers become freely available at all colleges and universities in the United States and that most students before graduating acquire a good understanding of their use. Only if we manage to bring up a computer-educated generation will society have modern computers fully available to solve its serious problems. While computers alone cannot solve the problems of society, these problems are too complex to be solved without highly sophisticated use of computers. I see three major bottlenecks that must be removed if this goal is to be achieved.

First, most university computation centers are still research-oriented. They are typically operated in a batch-processing mode with priorities given to a very small number of users who need a great deal of time. The philosophy of university computation centers must be changed.

Second, college administrations do not yet appreciate the immense favorable impact that a good educational computation center can have on their institution. I would like to propose that by 1980 no college or university should be given full accreditation unless computer services are freely available to all students. Use of the computation center must be considered the exact analogue of use of the library.

Finally, the implementation of this program for millions of students will take a great deal of money. In early 1967 the President's Science Advisory Committee published a report entitled *Computers in Higher Education*, which is known, after its chairman, as the Pierce Report. In great detail and most eloquently, this report made a case for recommendations similar to those I have just described. The committee also came up with a practical plan through which the United States Government could bring educational computation services to American colleges and universities. Unfortunately two administrations have failed to implement this report. Five years later the National Science Foundation was still receiving less than 10 percent of the funds recommended. Although NSF has done its best and has helped many institutions, what has been done is a drop in the bucket compared to what is needed.

Continuing Education

One of the greatest needs of our society is a far-reaching program of education in later life. Knowledge becomes obsolete at a rapid pace, often within a decade. In addition, people frequently want to change their field of work or to change specialties within a field. Also there is more leisure time available today than most people know how to use; devoting some fraction of this leisure time to continuing education could do a great deal to upgrade the level of civilization.

Men and women who can afford to return to their universities periodically for continuing education have, of course, the best of all possible worlds. But if this kind of education is to be made available to tens of millions of adults, much of it will have to take place at home. Once computer terminals in the home become common, a new dimension can be added to adult education.

In 1965, on the occasion of the dedication of the Kiewit Computation Center of Dartmouth College, I described my vision of adult education twenty-five years later. I still feel that the date 1990, which I chose at that time, was a fortunate one. Although everything I describe here and elsewhere about computer terminals in the home could be in effect by 1980, it is more likely that it will not become a reality until a decade later. This is not because there are any technological difficulties but because people have demonstrated discouragingly during the past decade that they are extremely slow in taking advantage of the potential of new technology. I see three major components in education in the home: (1) lectures over TV; (2) books; and (3) student interaction with the home computer terminal.

Many series of lectures have already been presented over educational TV. A surprising number of these are good and some of them are exceptionally good. With rapid improvements in the means of communication, it will be possible to have many channels dedicated to adult education. If not every adult American can return to the classroom, at least first-rate lecturers can be brought into his home. I mention books as an important ingredient to underline my guess that books will not be obsolete in 1990. Even with all the power of the com-

puter for information retrieval, I still think that the best
way to present large amounts of common material to all
students in a course is to print this material in the form
of a book. It is inexpensive, it is pleasurable, it allows
each student to proceed at his own speed, and there is
a special delight in the ownership of books.

These two ingredients exist today. However, they
allow only passive participation on the part of the student. Active participation is essential for first-rate education, and for this the computer will be necessary.
While the basic text material will be in the student's
hand in the form of a book, he will want to do supplementary research in a library. As I explain in Chapter
8, I am firmly convinced that by 1990 such research will
be accomplished by means of computers. Second, students like to have active interaction with their instruc-
tors. This is where CAI will come into its own. Although I have argued that CAI is a poor substitute for
a teacher, it is much better than having no teacher at
all. It can answer common questions on the part of
students and it can quiz the student on his understanding of the subject matter.

Once home terminals become common, TV lecturers
will be in a position to assign a wide variety of homework problems. Problems too simple to require the
power of the computer could still be corrected and
graded by the home computer system. And the availability of the computer would provide in each home the
kind of power that is now available to students at Dartmouth and a few other leading institutions. I am confident that by 1990 millions of Americans will have the
ability to do significant research in their homes. Indeed
this is a conservative prediction, since I have been doing
it myself for years.

I foresee a vast expansion in continuing education
through a combination of television, books, and home
computer terminals. A student wishing to take an ad-

vanced course will be able to rent a TV cassette containing the lectures, he can buy the books necessary for the course, and his computer terminal will provide him the power for research as well as testing him on his understanding of the subject matter. In effect, by 1990 every home can become a mini-university.

8
Library of the Future

Libraries are almost as old as civilization; indeed it is difficult to conceive of a civilized society without adequate libraries. Yet after thousands of years of successful existence, libraries may be becoming victims of the exponential growth of knowledge.

The Dartmouth College library collection doubled during the past thirty years. Although periods of slow and rapid growth alternated in earlier years, a doubling every thirty years describes the approximate average growth of the collection throughout its 200-year history. During the bicentennial celebration in 1970 the college acquired its millionth volume. If the same growth rate continues, the collection will reach 2 million volumes by the year 2000. Doubling present library holdings within the next thirty years, along with substantial increases in library facilities and staff represents an expenditure that the College cannot possibly afford. The problem is even more acute in larger libraries. Indeed, even if these libraries could afford to continue their growth, I seriously doubt whether a library of 10 million volumes can be used effectively.

At the same time there are ever-increasing complaints about the cost of dissemination of scientific information and the time lag between the finding of a result and its availability to the scientific community. The cost is a direct by-product of the exponential growth of knowledge. The earliest mathematical journal is less than 200 years old, but today several hundred journals are published in that field. To keep up with the most important current results the Dartmouth Mathematics Department subscribes to nearly 200 journals. Yet in spite of the tremendous mushrooming of scientific literature it is quite common to have a delay of as much as two years between the time an article is completed and the time it appears in print. In a less hectic age the two-year delay would have been insignificant but today it seems intolerable.

Finally, consider the problem of the research worker. It is an almost hopeless task to try to find out whether a particular piece of information has been published. A manual search of the journals can take an excessive amount of time and he can easily miss the relevant paper. Therefore, it is not uncommon for the same result to be published over and over again or for a searcher to waste valuable effort because of ignorance of an important result in his field. Therefore, active workers in scientific fields rely more and more on word-of-mouth communication and the assumption that if a given result sounds new to six key people in the field, there is a good chance that it is indeed an innovation.

So far computers have made virtually no impact on the dissemination of scientific information or on the storage of knowledge in libraries.

A National Automated Reference Library

In 1961, at M.I.T.'s centennial celebration, I proposed the creation of a national automated reference library.[1] Although in the past decade technology has changed greatly, and therefore many of the technical details of my proposal would have to be changed, I still believe in its fundamental philosophy. Let me consider first what such a library could accomplish and then how it could be implemented.

Let us start with the fact that in a typical million-volume library a high percentage of the books are rarely consulted. The duplication of these volumes in thousands of libraries is a tremendous waste of resources. Yet under the present system a good librarian has no alternative but to buy these books, since he has no sure way of judging exactly what his customers will need.

If, on the other hand, there were a fast and inexpensive way of obtaining access to a copy of a book which was lacking in a given library, the permanent collections of libraries could be enormously reduced. At the present time interlibrary loans are uncertain and slow. But suppose that a national automated reference library existed, from which any desired item could be obtained easily, inexpensively, and within a matter of minutes. Then the entire philosophy of what should be kept in permanent collections could be changed. Such collections could be limited to books that are used fairly frequently, which might mean cutting in half of the present size of large libraries. It would also allow a much slower growth in the future and therefore permit vast savings for the institutions that maintain the libraries.

The initial development cost of the national automated reference library would of course be great, and therefore I see it as necessarily a federal government project. However, I contend that it could be operated with a small fraction of the savings that the thousands of participating libraries would realize. This should make the project highly attractive politically.

I will further argue that an automated library could provide services that are not possible in traditional libraries. Once information is stored in machine-readable form, and a substantial time-sharing system is made part of the automated library, the entire problem of searching for relevant information takes on a new dimension. For the first time there would be hope that the scholar who is interested in the available knowledge on a specialized topic could systematically search all the available literature and find the items that are useful for his work.

Once society adjusts its thinking and habits to the availability of such an automated reference library, the entire practice of publication could also change. For example, there would be no point in publishing thousands upon thousands of scientific journals at tremendous cost and with all the delay involved in such publication. Instead, at very little cost scientific articles could be inserted directly into the automated reference library and be immediately available to anyone who cared to retrieve them.

We are once more faced with the problem of the correct division of labor between man and machine. While I anticipate the indefinite continuation of libraries organized along traditional lines, in the future they should contain only volumes suitable for direct human consumption—those whose immediate physical presence is desirable. I shall not attempt to deal with many necessary reforms—such as the need for regional, national, and international cooperation—but only with the creation of a computer-based information service. As I have indicated, I would envision the immediate insertion of a vast quantity of scientific results and other scholarly matter into computers in the national reference library. Human beings would retrieve from the computers only the minimum amount of information that a man-machine conversation determined to be relevant to their work.

New rules would have to be developed as to what should be kept in libraries. Items which are rarely called for, or whose importance diminishes rapidly, or which can be found only after a computer-aided search should be left to the national reference library. Any book that people are likely to read from cover to cover, such as a novel or a collection of plays or an interesting biography, should be available on the shelves. Similarly, any book of which a reader might want only a small segment but which is called upon regularly by hundreds or thousands of people should exist on the shelves. This would include such reference works as encyclopaedias, atlases, standard histories, and a variety of textbooks. For other works guidelines will be needed to determine what is kept in individual libraries as opposed to regional depositories. But no matter how these rules are interpreted, there will be a significant reduction in the holdings of most libraries.

The Problem of Storage

Is it really possible to store the equivalent of millions of volumes in an efficient computer-accessible manner? The answer to this is certainly yes.

For example, one technique, known as "ultra-micro-fiche," can store a volume of up to 1000 pages on a single 3-by-5 card. The volume can be looked at a page at a time by means of a reasonably inexpensive magnifying viewer. This means that 1000 miniaturized volumes can be stored in one ordinary card file a foot long, and several million in a large room. Moreover, there are now either available or in the experimental stage processes that will produce photographic images on a much smaller scale.

Before deciding how these millions of microform volumes are going to be stored, some consideration must be given to the manner in which the information they contain is to be retrieved. A million such volumes could be kept in 1000 card drawers, with the drawers numbered and the cards numbered within the drawers. The user could then find the catalogue number of a desired book and retrieve it by going to the appropriate drawer and thumbing through it until the desired card was found. Even this clumsy procedure would require less

time and effort than the standard procedure for retrieving a volume in the library. But, obviously, an automated system can do much better.

Although there are a variety of automated devices
that can pull out cards from a large collection, they are
usually not completely reliable and the cards are easily
damaged. Therefore a different kind of physical arrangement must be found. If the miniaturized images were
stored on a medium that is physically similar to the
magnetic tape used with modern computers, the 1000
volumes could then be stored on approximately 150
feet of tape, which can be positioned by existing devices to any one of the thousand volumes in just a few
seconds. (Such devices are relatively trouble-free, although tapes do wear out. However, the national library
could certainly afford to have backup tapes, so that
worn-out tapes could be replaced periodically.) In my
opinion, it is entirely feasible to have several million
volumes in automated form and to retrieve any given
volume or part of it in a matter of seconds.

The Problem of Search

The problem of finding relevant information is more
complicated. I assume that the automated library has
author, title, and subject catalogues in machine-readable
form and that these are part of a large time-sharing
system. If one desires to initiate a search by author or
title, the problem is simple. There is no difficulty in
storing the usual catalogue card information for each
author and each title and in retrieving all such entries.
The user can then look at the computer-generated list,
select the items he wants, and retrieve the desired books
expeditiously.

A search by subject, however, presents a much more
substantial problem. I may be able to tell the computer

that the book I am looking for belongs to the area of mathematics and, specifically, the subject of probability theory. But tens of thousands of books and journal articles fit that description. The last thing I would want is for the computer to give me a complete list of the authors and titles of all known works in probability theory. Somehow I must narrow down my search.

One can make a good start on this by providing a more refined classification system representing a great variety of topics and characteristics of books and articles. I could then engage in a discussion with the computer in which it could ask me a series of questions about my needs. For example, it might indicate a number of standard topics in probability theory, and I, in turn, would specify those relevant to my interest. Usually I would not be able to limit such a search to a single topic, and therefore the computer would have to do a very sophisticated job to avoid eliminating any items of possible interest. I might narrow the search further by telling the computer that I am interested only in items that were published, say, within the last three years. But the chances are that even at the end of a fairly lengthy conversation too many items that might be relevant will remain.

I therefore consider it essential that for every item in the library (considering an item to be an article or a chapter in a book) an abstract should be on file. While I visualize the books and journals stored as photographic images, I would like to see the abstracts stored in machine-readable form within the computer's memory. An abstract not exceeding 100 words for each item is still within the limits of what present-day technology can accommodate. If the subject-matter search was efficient enough to narrow the choice to ten or twenty items, the computer could simply present me with the abstracts of these items, and I could then choose those that sounded interesting.

Should this procedure fail, a truly sophisticated interaction between man and computer becomes necessary. Somehow I have to be able to tell the machine more specifically what I am looking for and ask it to search the contents of the abstracts for me. For example, I might tell it to look for certain key words or phrases in the abstract. Even this is not as simple as it sounds. One specialty in which I have done a good deal of research is the theory of Markov chains. However, I have to tell the computer that some authors will call them "Markov processes" and, to make life more difficult, the name "Markov" is sometimes spelled "Markoff." Considerable research will have to be devoted to the question of how such a conversational mode program can be written and how one can impart enough intelligence to the computer to enable it to be a truly efficient partner in the search.

Let me summarize how such a retrieval procedure might actually take place. I would sit down at a time-sharing terminal and call up the national reference library. After identifying me as a legal user (for the purpose of charging for services rendered) the time-sharing system would ask me a series of questions. Each question is designed to narrow down the search, and after each answer the computer would tell me how many items meet my conditions. First it would ask me if I know an author's name or a title; if I do not, it will start the fairly long process of determining the subject matter. When it runs out of suggestions, it will offer to search all remaining abstracts for key words and phrases. When I am satisfied that I have a sufficiently small group of items, it will furnish me with an abstract of each item. After supplying each abstract it will ask whether I am interested in this item. If I respond in the affirmative, it will look up the call number for that particular item and will request transmission of a copy of the relevant pages.

Once the search technique has been perfected, I am certain that a session of ten minutes at a terminal could accomplish more than hours of poring through library catalogues and thumbing laboriously through books.

The Problem of Transmission

Let us assume that a careful search has found three articles that a user wishes to read. For each article the time-sharing system has looked up the call number and has positioned the appropriate tape reader for the transmission of relevant pages. Now what happens?

One cheap solution would be to make a photographic copy of the pages and have it mailed to the user. But I am convinced that we can do much better than that. Why not send the photographic image directly to the user so that he will be in possession of a copy of the article within a matter of minutes? There is no doubt that today's technology makes such photographic transmission possible. The only question is whether sufficient band-width can be supplied to service thousands of users simultaneously.

Let us try to make an estimate of what the demand would be on such a national reference library. Suppose that we think of it initially as serving some 2000 college, university, and other research libraries. And let us assume that each of 400,000 scholars requests fifty pages per week. (I hope that this is a generous estimate of what the demand might actually be.) This would require the transmission of about 100 pages per second.

The problem of communication would be helped by the establishment of several branches of the national automated reference library, and the volume justifies it. As I indicated in Chapter 6, one could serve the whole United States efficiently with nine regional centers. Each of these would have a branch library, and I would add a tenth branch library in New England, since that region has a great density of libraries. The existence of ten branch libraries would cut down on the distance of transmission but it would still be necessary for each branch library to be able to transmit something like ten pages per second.

That volume is possible, but just barely, with present-day technology. It could be achieved by reserving one or more educational television channels for the national library, so that individual pages would be transmitted the way TV programs are now sent. Or they might be sent first to special distribution points via microwave circuits and then through less expensive circuits to individual libraries. Or, if even that is insufficient, satellites might conceivably be dedicated to the use of the national reference library. I do not claim to know what the ultimate solution of this problem is, but I am sure that there is one.

Let us return to the user who has identified three articles in which he has an interest and from which fifty pages have been transmitted to his local library. In what form should he receive these images? It was initially my inclination to say that they ought to be shown on a televisionlike computer terminal which he can read at his leisure. My Dartmouth colleague Robert Hargraves has, however, persuaded me that it would be much more efficient, and in the long run cheaper, simply to make a photocopy of each page, so that the user can take them home with him. Therefore, the result of his search will be, on the one hand, to find out what information is available, and on the other hand to obtain actual "printed" copies of those articles that he wishes to study at his leisure.

If such a system turns out to be practical, it would lead to an interesting twist on the present practice of publishing scientific work. Instead of publishing books and articles in large editions, most copies of which are never read, one copy of an article could be filed in the national library (or one in each branch library) and additional copies printed when somebody actually expressed an interest in reading the article. This may at first appear to be a wasteful method. No doubt the cost of obtaining a single item will be higher than it would be if the item had been mass-produced in printed form. But in that case it could be obtained only by subscribing to the journal, most of the articles in which might be of little interest. Most people would be happy to pay a premium for the computer's help in narrowing down their search to those items that are of conceivable interest, and for being able to put on their shelves only articles that concern them, rather than cluttering up their bookshelves with a huge collection of back numbers of journals. Moreover, in the proposed process one would be much less likely to miss important new results.

To complete the description of the retrieval process, through a conversational-mode use of time sharing the reader searches the collection of the national reference library for those items that are of current interest to him. When he has narrowed the search down to a reasonable number, he starts reading abstracts, still in time-sharing mode. He indicates those abstracts that seem worth following up, and these requests automatically trigger the positioning of tape readers to the indicated pages of the books or journals. These pages are photographically transmitted by TV or microwave to a device in his home which is something like a Xerox machine. Within a few minutes he should be able to leave the terminal carrying with him copies of the requested reference material.

Evaluation

The establishment of a national automated research library would add an important new dimension to the man-machine symbiosis. Human knowledge has grown to such vast proportions that no human being can on his own make use of it efficiently. Therefore the power of the modern computer is needed to extract from that vast store of knowledge those bits that will help the individual in his current work. In my proposed scheme the computer plays a triple role. First, it is the custodian of the catalogue of information and it helps to search that catalogue efficiently. Second, when there are too many items of possible interest, the computer engages the human being in conversation and helps to narrow the search. (This feature alone would justify the existence of the automated reference library.) Finally, once the desired items have been identified, the computer can quickly search through millions of volumes to retrieve them and transmit them to the user.

A number of interesting questions arise. For example, would this system eliminate the need for reference librarians? I don't think so. However, their role would change substantially; it would no longer be their job to find items for customers but instead to aid them in the computer search.

What would happen to the publication industry? As I have mentioned, I believe that a wide variety of different types of books would continue to be published. But I am sure that the existence of an automated library would significantly decrease the demand for printing. However, much of the time of publishing firms is spent in selecting and editing books, and the demand for these services will be as great as ever. Indeed, in a way the demand for editorial services will increase, since no item could be inserted in the automated library without a carefully written abstract and careful cross-indexing for the purposes of subject-matter search.

I am not worried about the future of editors and proofreaders, since they will be fully occupied in preparing materials for the automated library. The chief difference would be that the final copy of each manuscript, instead of being set in type and printed, would be photographed, miniaturized, and inserted in the computer's memory.

However, when I first published this proposal, I received a large number of letters from publishers and authors' agents who were greatly concerned about what would happen to royalties. The question of royalties is not serious in relation to scholarly reference materials. After all, authors of articles in learned journals normally do not receive any royalty. However, for those cases where this is a serious issue, I have a proposal. Today authors receive royalties on the basis of the number of copies of their books that are sold. My proposal is that, instead, royalties should be based on usage. The computer could easily monitor the number of times copies of a given article or chapter of a book are transmitted to a local library. Since there would be a user fee imposed for each transmission, part of the fee could be turned back to the author in the form of royalties. (This system would be similar to that of paying royalties for phonograph records used in broadcasting.) A not insignificant benefit from this procedure would be the fact that authors would get an accurate picture of how much their work is read. This would be much more accurate than today's system, since certain types of books are commonly bought but never read. On the other hand, for standard reference works a single copy in a library may be read by hundreds or thousands of people.

Perhaps the greatest benefit to society would come about if some authors found out that nobody is paying any attention to what they are writing, and therefore there would be a significant decrease in the amount of worthless material that is published!

A Word of Caution

Throughout this book I concentrate on the positive aspects of computers and automation. Other books have emphasized the dangers inherent in their use and misuse. But I feel that I must here insert a warning. Without proper safeguards, a national reference library operated by the federal government could become a dangerous weapon for the suppression of "undesirable" knowledge. For this reason alone it is imperative that thousands of other libraries continue to exist. And while the initial cost means that the plan can be implemented only by the federal government, once the national library is in existence, policy should be set and the operations supervised by a distinguished panel of librarians, publishers, and users, not by a federal agency.

9
Computers as Management Tools

Present Use

Although modern computers were invented for scientific purposes, it was discovered very early that they can be of immense help to business and industry. One of the lovely stories from the early history of computers is how IBM put one of its own computers out of business. Once IBM was convinced that its general-purpose (or "scientific") computers were well established, the firm decided to develop a special-purpose computer for business problems. However, the latter had a rather short life, because the general-purpose scientific computer turned out to be more efficient for business applications than the special-purpose machines.

Today it is quite common to see the same model of computer used by one institution for business problems and by another for scientific and research purposes. There are also many instances in which the same computer works part of the day on business problems and for the rest of the day is available for education and research. Indeed, under a time-sharing system the same computer can be used for both purposes simultaneously.

The most common applications of computers in business and industry today fall into a category that might be described as bookkeeping operations. For example, most payrolls in the country are handled by computers. This is an ideal computer application since it is purely mechanical, requires great precision, and is highly repetitive. In the case of salaried employees there is a large but simple data base and a straightforward algorithm for calculating monthly salaries and various types of deductions. Human intercession is needed only in rare cases. Names of new employees have to be added or those of former employees dropped. Occasionally— usually once a year—new salaries are entered. And sometimes the nature of the deductions has to be changed, when the government ups the social security deduction or when an employee acquires an additional income tax exemption. For hourly wages someone must enter the number of hours each employee worked; otherwise the process is just as automatic.

Many companies have successfully turned out automated payrolls for several years, on time, without errors except for an occasional human mistake. Other well-known successful applications are keeping the company's accounts, inventory control, employee records, and, in the case of colleges, the keeping of student records.

I can testify from personal experience that since Dartmouth College adopted its well-designed automated system of student records, both faculty and student complaints have diminished significantly. We get accurate and easily readable enrollment lists at the beginning of the term and again as soon as the period for student course changes has expired. Grades are entered simply and quickly, and students and their parents receive reports much faster and more accurately than under the manual system. In addition, new services have become possible. For example, the Mathematics Department now receives at the end of each year a record of all mathematics grades accumulated by students currently in college. This is of immense help in advising students and in writing letters of recommendation.

Even though most of these systems work very well, there have been a number of catastrophes. Companies have been known to accept the overoptimistic estimates of computer manufacturers as to the time it takes to install the new system and the cost of operating it. One hears of major organizations that are temporarily out of business because of the misbehavior of a machine. Even more often one hears of companies that have successfully converted to automated bookkeeping systems only to discover that they are now spending more money without any visible improvement in services. Such faulty management decisions accompany all technological innovations and cannot be blamed on the new technology.

I noted earlier that many of the popular complaints about machines are due to the fact that in the beginning companies used computers entirely to improve efficiency or to save money without regard to the effect on the services they provide for their customers. Several good examples are now available to illustrate that this also is poor management rather than an inherent shortcoming of computers. Banks and airlines were among the early sophisticated users of modern computers. They have made effective use of modern computers to cut down on their expenses and improve the accuracy of their record keeping. And they have been able to provide entirely new and desirable services to their customers.

Banks can now provide a variety of savings accounts and loan services (including automatic loans) to their customers. I am told that these services would simply not have been practical under a manual bookkeeping system. The efficiency of airline reservation systems has contributed greatly to the convenience of air travel. Recently I applied for a seat to Washington on a minor airline. I was given a confirmed reservation on a late flight and was wait-listed for the earlier, more convenient flight. By the time I arrived at the airport, the company's computer had allocated me a seat on the earlier flight, made available by a cancellation. I was indebted to the computer for a good night's sleep. And the airline was assured of both profits and good customer relations by having an airplane take off with every seat filled and no angry customers left at the foot of the ramp.

Management Information Systems

While the examples I have cited illustrate the great usefulness of computers for bookkeeping functions, so far the machines have had very little impact on the planning and decision-making functions of management. It is a sad fact that while most of these bookkeeping systems could be invaluable to management, they were generally designed for a narrow purpose and so provide little or no help in the broader functions.

An example from Dartmouth illustrates the difficulty. Fifteen years ago the college's Committee on Educational Policy became concerned as to whether engineering students were getting a sufficiently good liberal arts background. It was generally believed on campus that engineers do much worse in their English courses than non-engineering students. No doubt this was based on individual experiences where a student who did very badly in an English course was found by the professor to be an engineering student. It is typical of human beings that examples that support one's preconceived prejudices make a great impression, while those that contradict such prejudices are conveniently ignored. Two full professors were dispatched to collect data on the English records of engineering students. They worked very hard for two months, poring through handwritten records, to discover that the belief was totally groundless. There was no statistically significant difference between the English grades of engineering and non-engineering students; indeed, the English grades of engineering students were actually slightly higher than those of the rest of the student body. Today all these student records are kept in automated form, and one would like to believe that therefore the job done by the two professors would be much easier. Unfortunately this is not the case.

Keeping student records, like handling payrolls, is an ideal application for a batch-processing system. Very large amounts of data are processed in sequence, according to prescribed rules. In the case of student records, once programs for the addition of grades and the computation of term and cumulative averages have been written and debugged, these programs can be used over and over again. But they were not designed for research purposes, and one of the greatest disadvantages of a batch-processing system is the fact that reprogramming it is so time-consuming and costly.

Last year the same committee wanted to study the pattern by which students fulfill the foreign-language requirement. Although in a sense all the relevant information was available on a computer, the committee ran up against nearly insurmountable difficulties. For example, the computer does not recognize the term "foreign language," and even if that could be explained to it, it would not recognize the term "pattern." The committee could have obtained from it a listing of all the foreign-language courses elected by each of the 3200 undergraduates, but then these listings would require weeks of study before the desired information was secured.

We have a plan for solving this problem. Each year we will transfer cumulative student records from the batch-processing bookkeeping system to DTSS. We will take the records exactly as they are kept for normal operations, except that all student identifications will be deleted to protect the privacy of student records. We will rearrange these data into a form more suitable for educational research. Then we will write a set of programs that can serve as tools for anyone who wishes to conduct an educational study. Once the data are in convenient form, even if none of the existing programs will do the job, in a time-sharing system it is not difficult to write a new program to carry out a particular research project. For example, the program needed to study the patterns of language elections by students could be written and checked out by a single programmer in two or three days. This conversion process will change student records from a bookkeeping system into a management information system.

A similar process could be applied to the payroll, personnel, and accounting systems of companies. If the vast amount of valuable data contained in these files can be made available on a time-sharing system, it can be turned into a powerful tool for the management. But I suspect that the conversion in these cases would not be easy. Dartmouth's own accounting system was designed for a variety of purposes. First of all, it serves to control thousands of different budget categories. It leaves a trace for the auditors so they can reassure the Board of Trustees that no one has been stealing money from the college. It has to meet a number of requirements of the federal government to conform with the multiplicity of laws governing employment, tax deductions, and the control of federal grants. It was not designed to be particularly helpful for budgeting and long-range planning.

The distinguished American social scientist Herbert Simon, describing our dilemma as living in an "information-rich world," says that the problem is not one of insufficient information but is caused by the fact that we are completely flooded with information which we are unable to manage. It is thanks to Dartmouth's efficient computer bookkeeping system that we are able to maintain many thousands of accounts accurately, but it is also a by-product of the system that we have such a vast complexity of information about the finances of the college that human beings cannot cope with it without the aid of the computer. Simon's thesis is that a good information system should provide us, not with as much information as possible, but with the least information that serves our need.[1]

Since Dartmouth's accounting system is on a cash basis, the budget officer can easily check whether a given officer has spent more than seven-twelfths of his budget after seven months of the year have elapsed. But he has no idea whether commitments have already been made that will exceed the total budget. This is a typical example of a system designed for one purpose that fails to meet another equally important purpose. It is great for accounting purposes and very poor for budget control. Since an academic institution cannot assume that every faculty member with a research project, or even every departmental chairman, is an expert in accounting, this is a dangerous way of living. Indeed, we have to sweat out a two-month "closing of the books" at the end of every budget year before we find out whether we ended the year reasonably on target or with a huge deficit.

The purpose of a well-designed management information system is not to provide a great volume of information. The job of the computer is to store this great amount of information and to provide summaries to management as they are requested or when the computer spots certain danger signals that the management has asked to have monitored. For example, on the basis of expenditures plus commitments the computer should estimate what the annual expenditure in a given budget category will be. If this appears to be significantly over the budgeted amount, it should immediately notify the budget officer. The computer should also be able to provide summary information in any form requested, not simply in the form that some computer programmer thought would be convenient.

When I was elected president of Dartmouth College it was a common misconception that I would be much more sympathetic to the peculiarities of computers than most managers. Exactly the opposite is true. When we want to implement a new way of operating, I have no patience at all with the statement that "the computer can't do it that way." I know that such a statement is invariably false. What it really means is that the computer system was designed in too inflexible a manner and the computer programmers feel that it is too much trouble to reprogram.

An embarrassing incident occurred during my first year as president. I wanted to know what the potential effect of certain changes in patterns of giving would be on the annual alumni fund. My associates provided me with a beautiful printed table that listed for each class the number of donors for various sizes of gifts and the total amount collected from these donors. It contained far too much information for any human being to absorb. I therefore had to ask my secretary to take all that computer-produced information and type it back into the computer. It then took me only an hour to write an appropriate program and to obtain all the analysis that I desired. The moral of the story is that all that information should never have left the memory of the computer. It should not be the purpose of any information system to print enormous tables but rather to store them so that appropriate summaries may be computed from them.

A simlar experience relates to the annual exercise of promoting faculty members. For example, each year a list of associate professors who have been in rank a certain number of years is needed to assure that no possible candidate for promotion to the rank of professor is overlooked. While we have lovely computer-produced lists of all faculty members, with lots of information on them, until very recently a secretary had to go through the list to pick out the associate professors who had been in rank long enough to be promoted. This was not only time-consuming but resulted in embarrassing errors. We now keep a duplicate list in the memory of the computer and can produce the desired list, and others like it, in a minute.

What is needed to produce a useful management information system? Since most companies of reasonably large size keep vast amounts of information inside the computer, there is usually no lack of information. However, it is essential that, as information storage systems are designed, proper attention is given to the manner in which it will be desirable to retrieve the information. This requires that the management explain to the system designer the kind of information desired and the form in which it needs to be supplied. It also requires that the designer have sufficient imagination not to be bound entirely by the needs of the present day but to devise a system that is flexible enough for future needs.

In addition, a considerable training program may be necessary for those employees who generate information. It is no more time-consuming to provide this in a standard format that will make it useful throughout the institution, but it may mean changing old habits. Someone in authority may have to resolve jurisdictional disputes as to which of two offices will change its system of keeping information. And, most painfully, middle and top management will have to be trained to make use of all the information that becomes available. It is a simple economic calculation that a man who earns $25,000 a year cannot afford to spend a week doing by hand something that a computer can do in five minutes!

Models

Most sizable companies have effective automated bookkeeping systems. Some now have good management information systems available, and many more are in the process of constructing such systems. But to fulfill the needs of top management a third stage will be necessary. To the best of my knowledge no company has yet reached this stage.

What top management needs for long-range planning and effective decision-making is a model of the operation of the company. By a "model" I mean a theoretical description of how the company functions. This may consist of a set of formulas, or it could be in the form of a computer program. While an effective management information system is a necessary prerequisite for a model, it is not in itself a substitute for the model. Let me again illustrate the difficulty in terms of a concrete example. Dartmouth College is considering a plan of "year-round operation" under which we would add a summer term to our present three-term calendar. The crucial question that has to be answered is: If we add 1200 students in the summer to the normal enrollments in fall, winter, and spring, by how much will the expenses of the college increase? If we had an answer to this question we could compare it with the additional income that would be generated by the increased enrollment and come to a rational management decision. It is very frustrating to know that, although in a sense all the necessary information is contained in our computers, we will have to answer the question by means of educated guesses rather than a careful calculation.

I claim that no university has a clear-cut understanding of the relation between new educational plans and the resulting increased costs. For example, at Dartmouth we can easily compute the cost of the library per student, but this figure is totally meaningless. We maintain a superb library because our faculty and students expect such a library. If the enrollment was increased or decreased by a thousand students, this would have very little effect on the total library budget. On the other hand, if Dartmouth started a law school with one hundred students this would vastly increase the budget of the library.

We can calculate the number of additional faculty members we would need to accommodate a thousand more students. We can even make an educated guess as to how much additional office space and classroom space would be needed, but it would be no more than a guess, and perhaps a dangerous one. One has a strong tendency to assume that costs increase "linearly" (in proportion to numbers). I know that with the academic buildings now in existence or on the drawing board we can add twenty-five more faculty members without additional construction. But if we added fifty more, half the present academic buildings would be insufficient for the departments housed therein. And given the fact that faculty members in a given department wish to be housed close together, the resulting cost of construction would be staggering.

We have no clear understanding as to the effect of a certain number of added students and faculty members on the supporting staff of the institution and on the size of the administration. Since the supporting staff works on annual contracts, one might argue that there would be little additional expense in having a significant number of students on campus during the summer. But there is the danger that if maintenance of dormitories has to be squeezed into brief vacation periods a great deal of overtime would have to be paid to employees. These

are but a few of the unknowns that have to be answered
with educated guesses when one tries to make a cost
estimate for a new educational plan.

I feel a great need for a model of the operation of
Dartmouth College. Such a model would contain the
numbers of people in various categories, the physical
facilities, and the costs associated with these activities
by major budget categories. But, more significantly, it
would contain the dynamic interrelations among these
various factors. The model should contain formulas
which, given a proposed increase in the student body,
enable the computer to calculate the number of new
faculty members, the resulting need for greater facilities,
and in turn the supporting and administrative staff
needed to service these additional demands.

A modern time-sharing computer system is ideal for
the construction of a model. Such models are beginning
to have a major impact on the development of the social sciences. We can build within the computer an
image of the institution with a careful description of
how the various components of the institution are inter-
related. The difficulty in constructing such a model is
not a shortcoming of computers, or the problem of
writing a sufficiently sophisticated program, but our lack
of understanding of how an institution operates. That
such dynamic models of complex institutions can be
constructed was demonstrated by Jay Forrester.[2] No
doubt any initial attempt at such a model would be far
from perfect, just as Forrester's models are not perfect.
But the building of the model would force top management to state its understanding of the functioning of an
institution in terms sufficiently explicit to be converti-
ble into a computer program. And through use of the
model one would gain experience as to which assumptions are incorrect or incomplete and one could over
a period of years improve the model.

Forrester has demonstrated conclusively that intuition is a very poor substitute for a thorough understanding of the operation of a complex social system. It is my guess that a model of a university or of a major industry would, even in its earliest stages, serve significantly better for planning purposes than reliance on management's educated guesses. It is the only means I can conceive of by which one can anticipate catastrophes rather than waiting for them to occur.

How would such a model actually be used? Let us imagine a meeting of the board of trustees of a college or of the directors of a major company in the age of computer models. An officer proposes a new plan of action. The board must consider this as well as a variety of alternatives. There would be an expert sitting at a computer terminal to assist the board in its deliberations. During the discussion five different plans of action are proposed. Then and there the expert could enter these plans into the computer and ask the machine to estimate the relative costs of the courses of action and to inform the board of their various consequences. The final decision is still up to the board, but it would have hard facts on which to base it. A board of trustees of a college would not simply choose the cheapest course of action but rather weigh the relative costs and educational benefits. (Since in a well-endowed private educational institution even the student who pays full tuition pays only half the cost of his education, one might say that the best way the trustees can "maximize profits" is to refuse to admit any students.) Therefore the value judgments must be left up to human beings, but in the future these can be made after knowing all the relevant facts and all the consequences, both short range and long range, of a proposed course of action.

Once again, if a group of human beings acts as a team with a well-programmed computer, both can fulfill their roles more effectively than either acting on its own.

10
Computers in the Home

Is It Possible?

In an address at the dedication of the Kiewit Computation Center in 1965, I predicted that computer terminals in the home will be widespread by 1990. How feasible does that prediction look in view of what is known about computers today?

Suppose that we set an initial target of bringing computer service to three million homes. As I indicated in Chapter 6, nine regional centers would cover the United States efficiently, keeping the cost of communication within reasonable bounds. Therefore the average center would have to service some 300,000 customers; however, the key question in any time-sharing system is not how many users there are altogether but how many of them wish to use the system at any given time. If we assume that an average home will use its terminal an hour a day, it is reasonable to guess that at peak periods 10 percent of the users may be on simultaneously. Therefore a regional center must be able to handle 30,000 simultaneous users.

The easiest problem to solve is that of the computer memory. Since there are now on the market laser-beam memories that are able to store and retrieve efficiently the equivalent of 1000 sets of the Encyclopaedia Britannica, even today's technology is sufficient to solve the memory problem. On the basis of our experience with DTSS, the assumption that the average home would want a piece of the memory equivalent to ten pages of the Encyclopaedia Britannica appears to be a very generous estimate. That means that a 1000-encyclopaedia memory could accommodate over two million users! Even assuming that there will be enormous data files and highly complex programs available to the users of the system, I cannot see any difficulty in meeting the demand.

The communication problem presented by 30,000 simultaneous users is much more serious. While the number of telephones in New York City is much greater than 30,000, the typical telephone switching network is based on the assumption that a call will take minutes rather than hours. We had an interesting experience when the Kiewit Computation Center was under construction in Hanover, New Hampshire. The New England Telephone Company sent representatives for a courtesy visit to find out what kind of telephone service the computation center would need. When we indicated that in addition to our local users we hoped to accommodate fifty lines to schools in New England, they took that number very calmly. However, they then asked what the average length of a conversation was likely to be and our reply was "eight hours." The reply was perfectly serious, since the typical school calls the computation center in the morning and stays connected to the system until school lets out. That presented an entirely different challenge to the company, since there were only sixteen trunk lines going to White River Junction, Vermont, the major switching network in northern New England. We could easily have cut off some two million people from the use of long-distance telephones if sixteen of the schools called in early in the morning and stayed on the system throughout the day. With a year's notice, however, the telephone company had little difficulty in providing the additional capacity that we needed.

It is safe to predict that by 1990 computer communication will put a much heavier load on the communication system than all telephone calls combined. However, those who are planning the future of the communication system are well aware of this problem and I am confident that within the next two decades there will be an immense increase in capacity. All the necessary new technology exists today, although the installation of a vastly expanded national communication network, and much greater bandwidth for local communication, will be costly and time-consuming. This is one of several reasons why I consider 1990 a much safer date than 1980 as a target for computers in millions of homes.

Supposing that the problem of 30,000 simultaneous phone calls coming into a regional computation center has been solved, communication processors that can handle the load will still be needed. The flow of information comes in and goes out in "on/off" bits, with some ten bits per character. I know from my own experience that a speed of thirty characters per second is ideal for communicating with human beings. This is equivalent to about 300 words per minute. It is a great deal faster than people can type but is about as fast as one likes to receive information. Since much more material flows from the computer to the user than from the user to the machine, it is not uncommon for most terminals to be "outputting" at any given moment. Therefore we have to allow for a flow of about 10 million bits per second. Existing communications processors can handle a bit in about 10 microseconds, or 100,000 bits per second; therefore 100 communication processors would be needed for each center.

Let us make a similar estimate of the load to be put on the central processors. Here I have to make an assumption as to what the typical use of a large time-sharing network would be, and my assumption is that the typical user will make very modest demands on the power of the computer. The vast majority of users on DTSS will use 4 seconds or less of computing time in a 15-to-20-minute session. Even that is too high an average figure, since once there are millions of customers, the applications are likely to be heavily oriented toward communication rather than computation. I will therefore guess at an average of 5 seconds processor time in an hour session. Thus the simultaneous users will need 150,000 seconds in a given hour. To this must be added an allowance for overhead, which I will assume to be 100 percent. The need therefore is for about 100 hours of computation time each hour; in other words, 100 parallel processors.

However, I have made the preceding calculation on the basis of what computers can do today. While I have already indicated that I do not expect a spectacular increase in the speed of computers, it is perfectly reasonable to assume that by 1990 they will be ten times as fast as they are today. Therefore the entire load at the center could be handled by ten central processors plus ten communication processors. That is a very reasonable size for a multiprocessor center.

But can the cost be brought down to a level at which the average home can afford to have a terminal? In the area of costs my estimates are likely to be shaky. However if I am far wrong, I am likely to be wrong on the high side, since a major technological breakthrough may bring the cost down. If Dartmouth's computer center were operated as a commercial endeavor, it would have a budget of some $2 million per year. (The actual cost to Dartmouth College is much smaller.) The center operates with two central processors and two communications processors. Thus a center five times that large would need something like $10 million per year. However I am talking about future computers that will be ten times as fast. It has been the invariable experience in the past that, while faster computers cost more, they do not cost proportionately more. Therefore I will guess that in order to pay for the ten-times-faster computer the cost estimate will have to be multiplied by three, which will require an annual budget of $30 million. That is only $100 per customer per year. Thus it is reasonable to expect that computer service for about an hour a day can be provided in 1990 for about $10 (in 1971 dollars) per month. Even if that estimate should be too low by a factor of two or three, it still suggests strongly that we may expect to see computer terminals in homes by the millions.

One major bottleneck, which I mentioned earlier, remains—namely, reducing the cost of terminals. But by 1990, with a market of millions of customers, a reliable and attractive terminal will surely be within the means of the average family.

I therefore visualize nine regional centers initially, each with twenty processors, serving a total of three million customers. If the number of homes that desire such service should climb to, say, 10 million, I would suggest increasing the number of centers rather than increasing the size of each center. Having thirty regional centers could cut the cost of communication significantly, since centers would be available much nearer the customer. Such diversification would increase the efficiency of the over-all network and would make it easier for the various centers to provide "local" services.

An important and highly controversial question is whether it is more in the national interest to have a single computer network or to have several available. There is certainly an advantage in having more than one, since competition can improve the quality of service. On the other hand, having as many as ten national networks would confuse the average user and make each network less useful to him. Perhaps the right compromise is something like that which exists in commercial television. Three major national networks competing with one another may be an ideal number. One could even envisage a number of small local centers which subscribe to a national network service but also provide special services for their own regions.

What kind of services could such networks provide?

A Personalized Newspaper

One possible use of the home terminal illustrates the wide variety of information retrieval that can be made available in the home.

The New York Times is a magnificent national institution. Yet in many ways it is anachronistic in the computer age. It is too bulky, too impersonal, and often out of date by the time one reads it.

Everyone is familiar with the problem of bulk. Very few of the readers of The New York Times ever read all the articles in a given issue, even on a weekday. Because of the bulk one often overlooks an important news item, even though the search is helped by an index. And when one finds a particular item, one may have to search through a long story, turning several pages, until one has extracted the details of particular interest to oneself. I have often wished that I could have the option of either having more or less detail.

While for most purposes it is quite sufficient to read The New York Times once a day, there are important instances where this is inadequate. I would like to cite an embarrassing incident in my own life. In July of 1971 President Nixon announced that he was going to visit China. This was certainly the most important international news story in many months. I happened to be out for the evening and therefore did not hear his special news broadcast at 10:30 p.m. or the 11:00 p.m. news. The next morning I read The New York Times very carefully, but I had the early city edition, which is the one that reaches New Hampshire, and it contained no mention of the sensational news. Therefore, I found myself at noon on the day after the announcement in a large group where I was the only person totally ignorant of this development. In the age of computers one can certainly demand that the newspaper one reads twelve hours after a sensational development should contain the story.

Finally, there is the highly impersonal nature of *The New York Times*. By "impersonal," I mean that because the *Times* has to worry about the interests of hundreds of thousands of readers, it does not tailor its news service to my needs. I want to argue that it is entirely feasible today for the *Times* to provide personalized service for each of its readers.

Let us consider a system under which the *Times*, instead of publishing hundreds of thousands of copies, would store the same information in a computer memory tied into a national network, from which each reader could retrieve the items he wanted, in as much detail as he desired. I will describe first what would happen at the newspaper headquarters and second what an individual user would do.

Each reporter would file his stories by typing them directly into a computer terminal. The computer would provide a number of automatic services to make his life easy. It would justify all lines so that they come out roughly of equal length, correct simple spelling errors, and make it easy for him to enter corrections and improvements. These services are now commonly available on many time-sharing systems.

The editorial staff would monitor new stories as they were entered into the computer and make policy decisions on which stories to accept and how much detail to retain. The stories would then pass to a group of proofreaders who would make final corrections before each item was officially accepted into the current version of *The New York Times*.

The style of writing would be somewhat changed to

make articles suitable for computer terminals. Many terminals now have a display screen similar to a television screen. These can show roughly five paragraphs, or about one-third of a column of newsprint. Let us call such a unit a "frame." Reporters would write their stories in frames. Short items might fit entirely in one frame, while long items would start with a frame that summarizes the story and then branch to several additional frames which elaborate on details. Each frame would indicate what additional details are available in other frames to follow up the story. The fitting of the story into frames would be the job of the reporter, just as it is now his job to make sure that the beginning of each story contains the most important details (for readers who never read beyond the opening paragraphs) and that all newsworthy items are contained somewhere in the story.

The editor would do his cutting by eliminating the frames he thinks are superfluous. He would in addition classify a new story under major headings (similar to those now used in the daily New York Times index) and provide a brief title or headline for each story. Each story would have a time of entry associated with it, so part of the editorial staff could worry about obsolescence. For example, it would be easy to arrange that any story that had been carried for a full twenty-four hours was eliminated and even more frequent changes made as old versions of stories were replaced by new ones.

I estimate that all the news in the daily New York Times could be contained in five hundred frames. However, I would expect that once the cost of printing the newspaper is eliminated, the bulk could be increased tenfold at a surprisingly small cost. This would require about a million words of computer storage, which is a little over 1 percent of the storage available on the Dartmouth Time-Sharing System. The work of reporters, editors, and proofreaders would be actually simpler than it is today, and much of the remaining staff of a large newspaper would no longer be needed. Therefore the cost of "publishing" a personalized newspaper would be lower than the cost is today.

A reader sitting in his home could dial into his computer network and ask for his personalized New York Times. The computer would have on file those general topics which the user normally reads. For example, he might normally like to see what is new on the international front, in finance, and in sports. The computer would take these topics up one at a time. In the sports section, it would give the reader a choice of all the different sports covered in that day's newspaper. Let us say that the reader selects baseball and tennis. The computer would list all the available stories under baseball, which might consist of a description of all the games that took place within the last twenty-four hours, the standing of teams, and a number of background stories. The reader might choose to see a description of how his favorite team fared, the team standings, and the news story on Carl Yastrzemski. Each story would then be presented to him a frame at a time, and he could ask for more details or not as he wished.

After the reader has seen as much of the story as he wished, the computer, upon a signal, would automatically proceed to his next request, until he has seen everything he is interested in. A frame can be presented at normal reading speed on a quite inexpensive computer terminal. With a more expensive device the frame could appear almost instantaneously, and then the user would have the option of reading the frame carefully or merely scanning it. I would estimate that the typical reader would be interested in some twenty news stories a day and would want to look at one, two, or three frames for each one. In half an hour he would conclude a highly enjoyable and profitable personalized session with The New York Times.

I would like to summarize the advantages of this scheme. First, each reader has available to him at any moment, day or night, a completely up-to-date newspaper. It should be perfectly practical to have no more than an hour's lag between the occurrence of a news event and its availability in one's personalized newspaper. Second, the reader would select just those items that are of particular interest to him. This will save him a good deal of time and yet assure him that he does not miss any news that concerns him. He can read as much or as little of each item as he wishes. For some items he might just scan the first frame and decide that this is all he wants to know. On others, he could get as much detail as he wishes, much more than is now available in a newspaper. If a particular story is of long-range interest to him, he could have it typed out on his terminal or stored in his own personal file in the computer's memory for future retrieval. And he would have all these services available in his own home.

It may be objected that while this scheme sounds great from the reader's point of view, it would bankrupt the Times, which depends on its advertising revenue. But this need not be the case. The computer network would charge the user for various services and could pay a royalty to the Times for each access by a user. Given that the cost of production of the newspaper is reduced, and the cost of printing and distribution is eliminated, the Times may make a profit on "sales" alone. Nor is it necessary to eliminate all advertising. Classified ads could be well indexed and made available to any user who desired to see them. If that did not suffice, the newspaper retrieval program could be so written that between frames it presented ads. However, I would then hope that by paying an extra fee I would have the option of eliminating all advertisements.

I make this suggestion freely available to The New York Times. I suggest that if the newspaper adopts it, it change its motto to "All the news that you see fit to read."

Other Uses

I have so far described two major uses of the home terminal, one for adult education (Chapter 7) and one to provide a personalized newspaper service. With a little imagination one can think of a large variety of applications. I will suggest a few examples, and the reader can then add his own favorite proposals.

My sister says that she would love to see home terminals provide easy information on what is available in various stores. She wears rather narrow shoes and often has to go to a dozen different stores before she finds a single pair in her size. She would be grateful if before she left her home she could find out which stores have any shoes that might fit her, after which she could go to those stores and pick out a pair that she likes. We may assume that by 1990 even a small business will have its own terminal. Businesses could keep their inventory inside the memory of the computer, and any customer in the region could carry out a simple computerized search to find out what actually is available in a given store. As billing of customers will certainly be computerized by 1990, the computer would not only record a sale as a financial transaction but would automatically update the inventory of the store. Therefore a clerk or a customer could know immediately what is available, and when certain items are running low the computer could make out an order for replacements.

I am convinced that for items exceeding one dollar in price cash transactions will totally disappear. The multiplicity of credit cards is already a step in that direction. However, popular as today's credit cards are, the system is basically inefficient. You present your credit card in a store and sign a bill. This has to be sent by mail to an office of the credit card company, which then has to bill you and collect a check from you. In turn, that check is sent to your bank which transfers money to the bank of the credit card company which in turn pays the store. There is enormous waste in all this. As a matter of fact, I suspect that one reason credit cards are so popular is that it often takes as much as two months to receive a bill for a purchase.

A more practical system would be for each person to receive a credit card from his own bank. Purchases within the limits of the same regional computation center would then be very simple. When buying an item you would present your credit card for insertion in an appropriate computer terminal. This would automatically result in a credit to the account of the store and a debit to your account. If during the transaction you exceed your balance, a red light would come on and the sale would be refused. Or, more likely, the system by which banks provide automatic loans up to a certain limit for their customers will be expanded, so that moderate overdrafts would result in an interest charge rather than in the refusal of payment.

Most people would probably have two credit cards, one from their own bank and one from a national credit agency. The latter could be used outside one's own region. The national credit agency would provide a computer service which would channel a request from a far-distant location to the customer's own bank and provide temporary credit while the transaction was being completed.

A pleasant feature of this system would be the fact that it will not be necessary to balance one's checkbooks. This would be done automatically by the bank's computer, and the customer could call up on his home terminal at any time to find out what his balance is. Of course, many people are concerned about invasion of privacy and over the possibility of unauthorized persons using their credit cards. Depending on the cost one is willing to pay, there is no end to the safety features that can be built into such a system. For example, the computer would tell you your bank balance only if you call from your own terminal and provide an appropriate code word in response to a question. That system is probably as safe as a safety deposit box in a bank. A similar feature could be provided for the use of credit cards, so that an attempt to use the card without the appropriate code word would not only be useless but would immediately result in the arrest of the thief.

Let me speculate as to how each member of the family might use the computer terminal. Father, if he brings his work home from the office, can use the terminal in place of a sizable office staff. It can have access to the files of his company, it can help him in carrying out research, and at somewhat greater cost it could even transcribe letters and send them for him. (The delivery of the letter would consist of its being presented on the recipient's own terminal.) If he is interested in the stock market he can receive the latest quotations and enter a buy or sell order with his broker through the computer network.

Mother can do most of her shopping through a computer terminal. She can either find out what is available and go in person to make the purchase or actually enter her shopping list in the terminal. The list would be "delivered" to the local supermarket and the goods automatically packaged and loaded on the truck. She could plan her weekly menu in a simple session on the computer, providing not only variety but also a well-balanced sequence of meals, with special attention to the calorie intake of each member of the family. She would have immediate access to the listing of all forms of entertainment in the region, could choose the show she wants to see, find out what time it starts, and order tickets directly. If by 1990 the roles of man and woman have been completely reversed, the computer terminal will be equally happy to work out business problems for mother and to help father with his shopping and housework.

Children will find the home terminal an immeasurable asset in doing homework. Indeed the child of 1990 will find it impossible to conceive how the older generation managed to get through school without the help of a computer. After he or she completes all homework assignments, the computer terminal can serve as a major resource for recreation. Not only will the computer play a wide variety of games with the user but it can monitor multiperson games with each player sitting in his own home. It can deal cards or set up chess boards or enforce the rules of Monopoly. By that time, not only will two children in different homes be able to quarterback opposing football teams, but with televisionlike display terminals it should be possible to show simulated action so that the "quarterback" feels that he is in the midst of a huddle and sees what actually takes place.

All these services can be highly personalized at a relatively small cost in computer memory. Since we are allocating the equivalent of ten pages of the *Encyclopaedia Britannica* to each user, part of this memory could be earmarked for personal information on each customer, supplied by him or learned by the computer through experience. The computer would be happy to address the user by first name, nickname, or title, once the user's preferences are known. It could store the topics in the personalized newspaper that are of most interest to the user, as well as a list of his favorite sports. It could store measurements for various items of clothing to aid in computerized shopping. It could also keep a record of recently performed services so that the computer could "learn" its customer's preferences.

Through the use of such blocks of user information, many computer programs could personalize their services and make the use of the terminal both more efficient and more enjoyable.

The reader may feel that I have let my imagination run away with me, but all the applications I have mentioned are possible in principle today. Therefore they should be perfectly practical on a large scale by 1990. My list is likely to be deficient precisely because all these suggestions are already within the realm of possibility. I have made no provision for a multiplicity of new applications that will become reality within the next generation.

As I remarked at the dedication of the Kiewit Computation Center, not only do I foresee home terminals as commonly in existence by 1990, but I fully expect such advertisements as "Why walk all the way downstairs to use your friendly home computer? Get an extension for your bedroom!"

11
Solving the Problems of Society

I have presented the proposition that man has acquired a symbiotic partner. I should like to conclude with a consideration of some ways in which the symbiote might be used to improve the quality of human life.

Information Systems

In Chapter 9 I argued that in this information-rich world the techniques for providing management with the necessary information summaries are lagging behind the rate of collection and storage of information. If this is true for private companies it is all the more true for government agencies. Indeed, most bureaucracies are choking on the available information.

We seem to spend a major portion of our lives filling out long forms supplying government agencies with information. I cannot help wondering what happens to most of this information. I suspect that much of it is simply stored in filing cabinets that are seldom used but that help to justify the salaries of a large number of clerks. From the fact that different agencies of the same government ask identical questions over and over again it is perfectly clear that the various agencies are unwilling or unable to share information.

A great deal has been written and said about the dangers of a national data bank. We are all terribly sensitive about possible invasions of privacy.[1] I am not at all convinced that we are better served by having information in filing cabinets where all kinds of unauthorized personnel may have access to it than by having it contained in central data files with built-in safeguards against unauthorized use. To me the possible dangers of misuse of a computer data file are far outweighed by the fact that the current chaotic handling of information is a perfect excuse for inaction on the part of government bureaucracies.

There have been a number of articles in magazines and newspapers describing the incredible red tape that faces a new applicant for welfare aid. The usual excuse for this is the fact that a small percentage of welfare applicants abuse the system. Such abuse would be much more likely to be corrected by the existence of a centralized information system, which might indeed eliminate a small number of applicants who cheat, but would also remove once and for all the opportunity for welfare bureaucracies to give new applicants a run-around. The danger of knowing too much about a few of the applicants is far outweighed in my mind by the fact that a government inspector could quickly discover which welfare agencies are doing an atrocious job in helping the poor.

In a period of high unemployment national priority should be given to providing a first-rate employment service for all citizens. The present hodgepodge of state, local, and private employment agencies is totally unsatisfactory. Computers have made hardly any impact on employment services. At best, a few states are beginning to use batch-processing systems which produce reasonably up-to-date listings of jobs. However, the problem of matching individuals with jobs for which they are qualified, and which they can reach by reasonable means of transportation, is much too complex to be treated by a batch-processing system. It is an ideal application for a time-sharing network.

I can envision a time-sharing system under which employers could promptly list available job opportunities and remove jobs that have been filled. Applicants for unemployment could pay periodic visits to one convenient nearby office where a clerk could type in the applicant's qualifications and his preferences as to type and location of job. These could be instantaneously matched against the available jobs and interviews automatically scheduled. Such a system would remove the prejudices inherent in the personal interview technique and make accessible to each applicant a vastly larger number of job opportunities. It would also minimize the frustration of being sent to a distant location only to find that the job has already been filled.

There are additional benefits to be derived from a reasonable information system for welfare payments or for job matching. In the former example, the summary information provided by the system can be the basis for future legislation and for corrective action on the part of welfare agencies. In the latter, the information available in the job classification system could lead to the creation of new training programs, to attempts to import a certain type of industry into a given location, or to advising people with certain job aptitudes that employment opportunities in their field are much better in another part of the country.

The one area in which a substantial amount of cooperation has taken place is law enforcement. As a result of the vast increase in crime in this country, federal, state, and local agencies have shown unusual willingness to cooperate in the exchange of information. Martin and Norman have provided a good description of some of the progress made during the 1960s.[2] Even here, existing standards vary widely. The California system for providing instantaneous information on the possibly dangerous occupants of a suspicious car spotted by a patrol car is an outstanding example of a real-time information system. But there is room for a vast amount of progress before the full power of a modern time-sharing network is available to all law enforcement officers in the fight against crime.

Returning to the analysis of the development of information systems in Chapter 9, I note that although some painfully slow progress is being made in the creation of information systems for the use of government, the use of computer models for long-range planning is far in the future. The general tendency is still to attack each societal problem by launching a costly and time-consuming survey and then relying on statistical summaries for human planning. The need for these highly repetitive surveys could be removed by a good centralized data bank. Moreover, the statistical summaries usually throw away a vast amount of useful information. Averages of several different quantities surveyed may give no information at all as to the correlations among the variables. At best they may suggest such rough correlations as higher crime rates with densely populated poverty-stricken areas. Much more sophisticated computer techniques are needed to find all the factors that have an influence on the rate of crimes. Social planning today consists of well-intended guesswork on the part of poorly informed public officials. No major company could survive if its planning efforts were as haphazard and as unsophisticated as the planning efforts of most municipal agencies.

Simulation

Computers can serve as laboratories for the social sciences through a technique known as "simulation." [3] This technique was developed in universities and has received important applications to military planning but has had little or no application in civilian government agencies.

Traditionally laboratories contain scale models of complex physical systems. On a small scale model the laboratory scientist can study in detail the behavior of a very large system. From such imitative scale models scientists progressed to so-called analog devices. For example, electrical circuits were built which obeyed the same mathematical laws as mechanical systems and therefore could be used to study inexpensively the behavior of mechanical systems. Social problems, however, do not lend themselves either to laboratory models or to treatment by analog computers.

In a simulation laboratory a description of a complex system is built inside a computer. This is a fundamentally different concept than those employed in physical laboratories. Although such descriptions lack the precision of scale models or analog devices, they are much more flexible and are the best hope for attacking the highly complex systems that must be studied to solve problems of society. This technique can be illustrated in terms of the problem of traffic in a large city.

Suppose that the City of New York wished to make a significant improvement in the horrendous traffic in Manhattan. To build a scale model of the streets and traffic lights of the city, with thousands and thousands of cars, would be incredibly costly and much too clumsy. Neither is it feasible to design an analog computer that would realistically reproduce the flow of traffic. The building of a simulation model would be a major undertaking but it is entirely feasible. With a few man-years' programming effort one could describe to a large computer the physical layout of streets in New York, the placement and timing of traffic lights, the regulations governing the flow of traffic, as well as the traffic patterns observed at various times of the day and week in various parts of the city. One could then ask the computer to calculate the flow of traffic for a typical day or a typical week. No doubt the initial model would be unrealistic. With experience, adjustments could be made so that the computer would accurately reflect the actual experience in city traffic, including the traffic jams.

Such a model could be realistic only if it took into account chance events. While accidents occur in an unpredictable manner, they happen frequently in a large city and have a major effect on the flow of traffic. A great advantage of a computer simulation model is the fact that chance events can be built into it. There is a well-known technique for simulating random events on a computer. Let us suppose that we have reliable statistical information on the occurrence of accidents at various densities and speed of traffic. For example, on a limited-access road with rapidly moving high-density traffic we can expect one accident for each 100,000 cars. The computer model will then produce such accidents with the right frequency but at totally unpredictable random moments, just the way they actually occur.

It will be a costly and time-consuming job to adjust such a model to the point where it realistically reflects current conditions. However, once the model exists, the city has an incredibly powerful planning tool. Anyone who has driven in Manhattan in recent years knows that the city is using all of us as guinea pigs in its periodic experiments in trying to improve the flow of traffic by adjusting traffic lights, adding new lights, or increasing the number of one-way streets. These experiments can be highly frustrating to the driver, and the city has to wait several months until it has enough information to determine whether the experiment was at all helpful. Such an experiment could be replaced by a few hours' work on the computer.

City planners could suggest improvements in traffic regulation to be fed to the computer. It would then simulate several weeks of traffic and predict just what the effect would be if the plans were tried out. Since an entire new plan could be tested on the computer in a matter of an hour, planners could try out hundreds of different ideas until they came up with one that seemed to make a significant improvement in the flow of traffic. This would not only speed up improvements but remove the necessity of using thousands of human guinea pigs.

The simulation planning model becomes particularly important when major changes are considered. The necessity of expanding a major road in the Bronx has for several years created daily traffic jams that have led motorists to question whether the expansion was at all worthwhile. A good computer model could have predicted these traffic jams, and the city could have taken measures to avoid them.

The model could also be used to make sure that for a given number of dollars expended in improving roads or in building new roads, a maximal effect in relieving traffic congestion would be achieved. It could enable the city to estimate the costs of alternative means of transportation, such as the often-proposed plan of barring private automobiles from entering Manhattan but providing spacious parking garages just outside and a convenient mass-transportation system for entering the city.

Some excellent examples of the use of computer models for social planning are found in the work of Jay Forrester.[4] City planning, the planning of a mass-transportation system, pollution control, and similar problems are much too urgent and too complex to be left to amateurs to try to attempt to solve by a combination of intuition and paper-and-pencil calculations. By ignoring the power of the modern computer as a planning tool we are throwing away the most potent weapon available for an attack on perennial social problems. I am not suggesting that computers alone will solve the problems of society, but I am convinced that these problems cannot be solved without intensive and sophisticated use of the high-speed computer. Such problems are ideal illustrations for the main theme of the book—that man working in partnership with a computer can achieve vastly more than either can achieve on his own.

A major difficulty in implementing these ideas is the lack of trained personnel. We have available on the one hand a large array of social planners and on the other hand a small army of computer programmers. But neither of these groups on its own has the necessary expertise to build sophisticated computer planning models and the two find it extremely difficult to communicate with each other. I see the need for the development of a new type of professional, one who might perhaps be called a social analyst. Such a person would combine a good foundation in the social sciences, a thorough understanding of the use of basic mathematical and computer techniques, and an understanding of the behavior of complex systems. Forrester's work has shown that although the complex systems of society are qualitatively different in behavior from the systems of physics and chemistry, they show a great deal of resemblance to these systems. Therefore it is conceivable that, as a physicist develops an intuition of physical systems, a social analyst may develop an intuition for these new complex systems that we now find highly counterintuitive. His experience in planning a mass-transportation system may be transferable in part to long-range planning for a university or to pollution control.

I see a dual challenge to colleges and universities. Since most of the know-how in devising imaginative new computer techniques and in the study of complex social systems lies in these institutions, they could play the role of "think tanks" for society. Until the new professionals come along, the universities could put together teams that jointly have sufficent expertise to develop models of complex systems. At the same time they could launch training programs for future social analysts who could work as apprentices in these think tanks, acquiring a broadly based training that no one has at the present time. Only through such a two-pronged attack can I see the full power of the computer being applied to the solution of the problems of society.

Control Systems

Closely related to the development of planning models is the design of control systems. Let me illustrate this problem also in terms of city traffic.

It is a common experience to have to wait several minutes at a traffic light when no cars are coming in the opposite direction. This is annoying but not catastrophic. However, the typical experience during rush-hour traffic in Manhattan, where traffic lights are regulated according to a hypothetical traffic flow without taking into account what is actually happening, is truly disastrous. Cars going across town succeed in getting past a given traffic light and then are stopped in the middle of an avenue, blocking uptown traffic, because cars are backed up all the way from the next traffic light. As a result, traffic does not flow in either direction at the busy intersection.

It would be relatively simple to design monitoring devices to provide feedback to the nearby traffic lights. Even better, a computer system could control all the traffic lights in Manhattan and base its decisions on current information on traffic flows and traffic jams. For example, such a system would change the lights on a one-way street, not simultaneously, but in succession, in such a manner that the crosstown traffic that has gone past one traffic light would be allowed to continue until the computer was informed that the avenue was clear for uptown and downtown traffic. The cost of such a system would not be prohibitive, but it would require a

highly sophisticated computer design—a one-shot invest-
ment, not a continuing expense. One major benefit of
such a system could be an automatic control at bridges
and tunnels so that if Manhattan is hopelessly jammed
no more cars would be allowed to enter the island.

A good example of such a computer control system
can be found in any nuclear power plant. The chain reaction that is the source of energy must be controlled by
periodic insertion and removal of materials that absorb
particles. Due to certain unpredictable forces in such a
chain reaction, the control must be done with split-
second accuracy in order to sustain the chain reaction
but prevent a nuclear explosion. No human being could
possibly carry out this task, but a human-designed computer system handles it with great efficiency. Similarly,
the control of traffic is beyond the capabilities of even a
large number of police since they could never evaluate
the total pattern fast enough to take effective action. But
it could be carried out by a human-designed computer
system.

Another potential example of a computer control
system is the regulation of the quality of air and water.
These could be continuously monitored by automatic
sensors, with all the information being fed into a central computer. Such a computer could issue suggestions
for corrective actions before the air becomes unbreath-
able or the water hopelessly polluted.

A Proposal

At a lecture series sponsored by Johns Hopkins University and The Brookings Institution I made a more
radical proposal.[5] While I believe that in the long run
universities can play an important role in developing
new techniques for dealing with problems of society and

in training the necessary experts, I feel that more immediate steps have to be taken.

I proposed the establishment of a national computer development agency, a federally subsidized private agency that would develop computer systems for public use. The idea arose out of the fact that the needs of various governments are quite similar. There is neither enough money nor enough computer expertise for each city and state government to develop its own computer system. The agency would be concerned with the design, development, and testing of new systems on an experimental basis, as well as with training employees of local and state governments in the installation and adoption of such systems. I estimate that a significant program could be financed if local and state governments were charged a nominal per capita fee to be matched by a federal contribution. I recommend the idea because while the actual operation of the computer systems should be reasonably economical, the development cost may be several times the annual operating cost. A cooperative effort spearheaded by the federal government could distribute the cost of development of such systems among hundreds of local governments and dozens of states.

I am convinced that such an agency pledged to alleviation of social problems would be able to attract a large group of bright and dedicated young men and women. In addition, the universities, which are increasingly dubious about serving as think tanks for the military agencies, would welcome an opportunity to participate in a project of great social significance.

Let me return to my example of a traffic planning model and control system. If such a system were developed for Manhattan, it would be applicable with relatively simple modifications to all major cities in the nation. Therefore it is not fair to use the tax revenue of a single city to finance the major development effort. Nor can one expect that cities will have on their staffs sufficient numbers of experts to launch such a project. There is also the danger that a city may be pressured by a computer company to design a system highly profitable to the company but far from ideal for the needs of the city.

The federal agency could insist that all systems developed under its auspices would be usable on the hardware of any computer manufacturer that is willing to meet a few federally set standards. The program could be written in one of several generally accepted computer languages and use simple conventions to tie in with computer memories and control devices. Then a city would have the assurance that if it is not satisfied with the performance of the equipment supplied by a given vender, it could shift the entire system to the equipment of a different company.

The creation of such an agency could be the single most practical and effective step to assure rapid progress in applying computer systems to the problems of society.

Effect on the City

I have concentrated my discussion so far on the direct effects that the computer age could have on the problems of society. However, it is conceivable that the indirect effects may be much more dramatic.

It has been said that the vast increase in population, resulting in enormous concentrations in central cities, has caused the current horrendous problems of urban life. However, that description is far from accurate. The problems became particularly acute in the 1960s; yet in that decade there was little or no increase in the population of central cities; most of the increase took place in suburban areas. Therefore I conclude that the real source of the problem is not the increasing density of population in the cities but the vast daily movement of people in and out of the city. It is my contention that through modern means of communication and modern computer systems, it may now be possible to reverse this trend.

Historically cities have arisen as centers of manufacture and trade. Their importance as manufacturing centers is rapidly decreasing. As the cost of transportation has dramatically decreased, most manufacturers have found it advantageous to decentralize their manufacturing operations and to move them out of the congested and highly expensive areas of the central cities. Cities are now primarily centers of trade. But even the meaning of the phrase "trade center" has changed dramatically.

The early cities served as marketplaces—that is, places where goods were physically exchanged. Except in supplying the daily necessities of the residents of central cities, this role as a marketplace has mostly disappeared. We may still use such phrases as "I went to the city to buy a car (or a refrigerator)", but the phrase is highly misleading. The chances are that the transaction consisted of going to a store or showroom that has a few samples on display and a catalogue from which the order may be placed. The actual exchange of goods may be the shipment of the car or refrigerator from a remote warehouse to our home outside the city, an exchange for which we gave the store a check which might represent the yield of a sale made in a completely different location. No goods actually changed hands within the city itself.

This description is even more universally true when we speak of very large transactions. Cities still are the locale where major commercial transactions take place, but these are almost invariably paper transactions. Two individuals may sit down to "close a deal." However, all that happens is an exchange of information as to what one company is able to supply and what another company needs. If they can agree on appropriate financial arrangements and a timetable for delivery, the deal is closed. The actual transfer of goods will take place in one or more remote locations.

It is my thesis that the traditional role of cities as centers of manufacture and trade has changed to a role in which the primary purpose of cities is as a center for the collection and exchange of information and the carrying out of paper transactions. Perhaps the most dramatic example is the stock market. Vast fortunes are made and lost on the stock market and entire companies may change hands. However, the stock market itself is not the place where physical goods change hands; it is usually not even the place where paper certificates are exchanged. Its service is the collection and dissemination of information.

It is worthwhile to analyze the reasons that millions of people rush into central cities each morning. Some of this manpower is necessary to staff the remaining manufacturing installations, but these are rapidly deserting the major cities. Some of it is necessary to maintain the life functions of a city with millions of people. But the major fraction of the daily in-and-out movement is attributable to executives, professionals, and white-collar workers who staff thousands of offices located in the cities. Why is it necessary or desirable for them to make a daily pilgrimage from their homes to the city?

One reason is the desire to talk with colleagues in the same office or to counterparts in other offices. An increasing percentage of this talk is now carried on over the telephone. I have heard executives complain that they rush into their offices and then spend half their time talking on the telephone, something they could have done equally well from home. Second, they go to the office because that is where all the necessary information is contained in a vast array of files. Finally, they go to the office because their secretaries and assistants come to the same office and it is a convenient place to meet.

I predict that a dramatic effect on the pattern of employment and location of offices will come about by the widespread use of video telephones. I myself prefer a face-to-face conversation to a discussion by telephone. However, I feel that with the existence of video telephones conversations and small group discussions at remote locations will be almost as effective as face-to-face discussions. Very often I have to go to New York to attend a small committee meeting and perhaps have half-hour conversations with two individuals. It would be a vast saving of money and time if an appointment could be made for a conference video-phone call for the committee, and appointments for half-hour video-phone conversations in place of in-person appointments. We could still see each other's facial expressions, establish rapport, and share written documents or pictures, without having to leave our homes or offices. It is highly discouraging to note that, when one is "on the road," one spends a great deal more time in traveling (and waiting) than in actual useful work. I would much rather pay for an extensive video-phone conversation than to have to pay the cost of transportation, hotels, meals, and so forth. Most important, if social patterns change in the manner I have described, many of the reasons for rushing into the city will disappear.

A second major reason for going to the office is the fact that that is where the files are. However, I have previously argued that such information will in the future be kept in national computer networks. Once this occurs, the files of a company will be accessible and updatable from any location in the country.

That leaves only the last consideration, that of being where one's secretary and assistants are. I for one sincerely hope that computers will never replace secretaries. With a sophisticated computer system the job of secretaries can be made more pleasant and they can perform more functions in a given period of time. But I am convinced that a man-machine system is vastly more practical than a totally computerized system. With such a system secretaries will have automatic means of making corrections in drafts of letters and of producing several copies in slightly different format. The filing will be totally computerized and the retrieval process will be facilitated by a time-sharing system. But I will still find it more pleasant and more efficient to give my request to a human secretary who knows the peculiarities of the system rather than to battle with it myself.

Another possibility accompanying such changes is that all enormous office complexes will disappear. There is no reason why each executive could not pick a site for his office near his home and recruit secretaries and assistants from the immediate vicinity. The small offices would be linked by means of the national computer networks and the network of video-phones. Such an arrangement could greatly reduce the ridiculous amount of traveling that Americans take for granted. An eight-hour working day could be eight hours plus five minutes travel in the morning and five minutes travel in the evening rather than the eleven-hour day necessitated by the daily battle of getting to the office and coming home. Human beings would then have much more freedom in deciding where and how they want to live their lives.

This arrangement could also eliminate most of the relocation problems caused by large companies' transferring key people to various parts of the country. Someone living in Minneapolis could perfectly well carry out a task for a Kansas City office. He could keep the physical location and supporting staff to which he was accustomed and still function very efficiently for a central office many miles away. As long as that office is equipped with several video-phones and terminals giving access to one or more national computer networks, its exact location is irrelevant.

It is my conviction that if the need for millions of people to rush in and out of the city every working day is removed, we would be well on our way to a solution of urban problems. What exactly would be the role of the central city? Perhaps it will become truly a center for information where the machines are located but not the human beings who use them. It would still need a substantial staff of supporting technicians to look after the machines and the usual services necessary to support the people living in the city, but the density of population could be substantially decreased. Since the location of offices would become a matter of little concern, effective city and suburban planning could take place. Since cities still would have a central location, easily accessible, they might expand their role as centers for recreation and entertainment. Cities may become important because of the presence of museums, theaters, concert halls, and sports arenas, and as places of living for those who insist on seeing a play or a sports event in person rather than watching it over television.

I am making these predictions through a clouded crystal ball. I am not sure that the situation I have just described will actually result from new means of communication and computer networks. But these technological developments will certainly bring about a fundamental change in life styles. Therefore it is a major mistake to make plans for the solution of social problems on the assumption that society will in the future be organized in exactly the same way as it is today. For the first time in human history we have an opportunity for significant social planning. We cannot afford to waste it.

Symbiotic Evolution

Biologists have recorded many examples where a species threatened with extinction managed to survive by means of a significant evolutionary change. The human species is now threatened with extinction. The population of the world is increasing so rapidly, the means of mass destruction have become so horrible, natural resources are being used up at such an alarming pace, and man is polluting the environment so fast that we have at most a century in which to change the very texture of human society. Given the rate of human reproduction, a century is much too short a period for the usual forces of evolution and natural selection to bring about a significant change. Our best hope therefore lies in a new kind of evolutionary process which I have called "symbiotic evolution."

I have argued that in high-speed computers man has acquired an important symbiotic partner. We can help computers evolve by combining them with modern means of communication into national or world-wide computer networks. Time sharing provides the opportunity for man-machine interaction, so that man and computer and the communications network can all work together. It is my hope that through this partnership man himself will evolve without having to wait for the slow processes of biological change to take place.

The mere existence of computers increases man's intellectual capabilities manyfold. The existence of computer-communications networks will enable human beings at widely separated locations to function as a team. The vast capabilities of computer memories will enable us to make effective use of the explosion of human information and knowledge. The combination of these factors will enable us to solve social problems that now look almost hopeless.

However, this evolutionary development is only possible if man is willing to make drastic changes in his life style and in his conception of his own goals. A human being trying to solve a complex problem with his own resources will soon look as foolish as one trying to do the work of a bulldozer with a toy pail and shovel. Man must be willing to be freer in the sharing of information and in participating in team efforts where his partners will be both human beings and computers. We must rethink our entire educational system in order to train the next generation, not for the jobs of the past, but for those that are likely to be significant twenty years from now. Since it is unlikely that any educational system can provide a training that will see us through a lifetime, we may have to devise a system in which learning continues throughout one's productive life.

Nor will these changes in themselves solve our most critical problems. The computer may help to explain why the present population explosion cannot possibly be allowed to continue, but the decision to limit the growth of population must be made by man. The computer may help us to design ways of utilizing natural resources that will insure a long-range supply and also minimize pollution of the environment, but man must still decide that he is willing to sacrifice some luxuries and conveniences in order to protect future generations. Computers have already shown (in simulations by agencies of the Defense Department) that wars fought with nuclear or biochemical weapons would inflict damage from which the world might never recover, but man must still decide that he is ready to live in peace with his neighbors. New sophisticated planning models may help us to see the way toward eradication of disease and poverty and social inequities, but the few must still be willing to make sacrifices in order to help the many.

In short, the symbiotic evolution which I foresee will not in itself bring about the good will and dedication that are necessary to reverse the disastrous trends that now threaten our species. But without the potential contained in this symbiosis, good will can do little to alleviate our problems. The best-intentioned people, if they lack the technical expertise and the tools to achieve our goals, can make the situation worse instead of better. Therefore we must look to the coming of a new man-computer partnership to provide the means which, combined with sufficient concern by men for their fellowmen and for future generations, can hopefully bring about a new golden age for mankind.

Reference Notes

1. A New Species Is Born

1. Lynn Margulis, "Symbiosis and Evolution," *Scientific American*, August 1971.
2. James Martin and Adrian R. D. Norman, *The Computerized Society* (Englewood Cliffs, N.J.: Prentice-Hall, 1970).
3. John von Neumann, *Theory of Self-Reproducing Automata* (Urbana, Ill.: University of Illinois Press, 1966).

5. Symbiote or Parasite?

1. For a good discussion of these problems, see Martin and Norman, *The Computerized Society*.

7. Computers in Education

1. A useful summary of the current state of CAI can be found in Martin and Norman, *The Computerized Society*.

8. Library of the Future

1. John G. Kemeny, "A Library for 2000 A.D.," in Martin Greenberger, ed., *Management and the Computer of the Future* (Cambridge, Mass.: M.I.T. Press, 1962).

9. Computers as Management Tools

1. Herbert Simon, "Designing Organizations for an Information-rich World," in Martin Greenberger, ed., *Computers, Communication and the Public Interest* (Baltimore: The Johns Hopkins Press, 1971).
2. Jay Forrester, *Urban Dynamics* (Cambridge, Mass.: M.I.T.

Press, 1969) and *World Dynamics* (Cambridge, Mass.: Wright-Allen Press, 1971).

11. Solving the Problems of Society

1. See Martin and Norman, *The Computerized Society*.
2. Ibid.
3. John G. Kemeny, "Games of Life and Death," *Random Essays* (Englewood Cliffs, N.J.: Prentice-Hall, 1964).
4. Forrester, *Urban Dynamics and World Dynamics*.
5. John G. Kemeny, "Large Time-Sharing Networks," in Greenberger, *Computers, Communications and the Public Interest*.

Index

About the Author

Mathematician and philosopher John G. Kemeny, president of Dartmouth College, has pursued his dual interest in the sciences and the humanities throughout his career. Born in 1926 in Budapest, Hungary, he was brought to this country by his parents in 1940 to escape the Nazi tide. Knowing virtually no English, he enrolled in a New York City high school and graduated first in his class. He later graduated *summa cum laude* from Princeton on schedule despite a year and a half out for military service. While working on his doctorate in mathematics, which he received from Princeton in 1949, Dr. Kemeny was research assistant to Albert Einstein. He then joined the Princeton faculty and taught both mathematics and philosophy.

As chairman of Dartmouth's mathematics department for twelve years, Dr. Kemeny was a prime influence in developing computer time sharing as an educational tool. In addition to serving as president of Dartmouth, he holds the Albert Bradley professorship for innovation in teaching. He has become fascinated with the growing potential of computers and is convinced that knowledge of the computer should be an integral part of liberal learning. At Dartmouth he created a course on how the computer may effectively help solve problems of our technological society.

Dr. Kemeny is co-inventor of the widely used computer language BASIC. He is the author or co-author of twelve books, including *Introduction to Finite Mathematics* and *A Philosopher Looks at Science*.